# Remembering
# AMERICUS
## Georgia

# Remembering
# AMERICUS
## Georgia

### Essays on Southern Life

ALAN ANDERSON

Charleston    London

History
PRESS

Published by The History Press
Charleston, SC 29403
www.historypress.net

Copyright © 2006 by Alan Anderson
All rights reserved

*Cover photo:* 1894 photo of Windsor Park, county courthouse and jail city hall and
water tower, taken from the Windsor Hotel tower.

First published 2006

Manufactured in the United Kingdom

ISBN 1.59629.131.1

Library of Congress Cataloging-in-Publication Data

Anderson, Alan, 1951-
 Remembering Americus, Georgia : essays on southern life / Alan Anderson.
 p. cm.
 ISBN 1-59629-131-1 (alk. paper)
 1. Americus (Ga.)--History--Anecdotes. 2. Americus (Ga.)--Social life and
customs--Anecdotes. 3. Americus (Ga.)--Biography--Anecdotes. 4. Sumter
County (Ga.)--History--Anecdotes. 5. Sumter County (Ga.)--Social life and
customs--Anecdotes. I. Title.
 F294.A5A53 2006
 975.8'913--dc22
                                    2006012654

# Contents

# Acknowledgements

A work of this sort certainly requires the efforts of more than one person. While the writing is all mine, the compilation would have been impossible for me to do alone. I developed a love of history while growing up most of my life in the South. My parents, Command Sergeant Major and Mrs. A.M. Anderson, were both students of history, with my father concentrating on the Civil War in spite of his birth in Scotland. My mother's sister, Rosalie Purvis Bass, was herself the family historian and was always a wonderful background source during my years of research. Her son, J.T. Bass Jr. (better known as tbass), is a webmaster extraordinaire whose technical skills actually made this book's series of essays possible. Since becoming the archivist of the Sumter Historic Trust, Inc. in 1985, I have enjoyed working with the members in their support of historic preservation, especially in helping to finance our website, www.sumtercountyhistory.com. In general, I would like to thank all of those in our community who shared their stories, photographs and encouragement, with special appreciation for my cousin, R. Lee Kinnamon, who has always generously shared his treasure trove of family history memorabilia. I specifically want to thank the personnel at the courthouse, city hall and Lake Blackshear Regional Library who have put up with my constant requests for access to public records and the library's incredible microfilm collection. Finally, on a more personal note, this journey of discovery has been shared, and inspired, by my loving wife, the former Jennifer L. Hicks of Ellaville; my sister, Mary Jo Anderson, a superb public school teacher; my brother, David A. Anderson, who has perpetuated the family name with his two sons, William Alexander "Andy" and David Andrew Jr.; and my best friend since college days, Johnny M. Burnette.

# Introduction

The history of Americus and Sumter County is truly representative of Southern culture in general. From its pioneer era to the present, whatever happened here was typical for the state and region as well. Any student of American history will gain insights and benefit from reading these essays, as the South did not develop in a vacuum. A veritable plethora of primary and secondary sources are quoted extensively throughout the series. As a teacher of Georgia history for a quarter century in the local public school system, I always pointed out to my students that we can never truly understand the present without first studying the past. The past, after all, is prologue to the present.

# A Short History of Sumter County

As students of history it is incumbent upon us to conduct our research as thoroughly as humanly possible. Primary sources, such as first-hand accounts by eyewitnesses, are especially valuable in this respect. This essay, gentle reader, gives you a unique chance to compare and contrast two such examples. The first is by Joseph Absalom "Nap" Cobb and the second by his mother, Mrs. Jane Moore Wheeler Cobb. The former appeared in the *Americus Daily Press* of December 16, 1902, and the latter in the *Sumter Republican* of June 6, 1884. Both parties can be seen in the accompanying family portrait.

> *Shortly after the treaty with the Creek Indians, made at Indian Springs, on the 12th of February, 1826, and was ratified April 22nd of the same year by the government, Lee county was laid off and surveyed and divided into districts and lots. The land was drawn for in 1827, when Jacob W. Cobb drew lot No. ____ in what is now known as the 28th district, and the following year he and Avery Wheeler moved to it, it being situated on Line creek, or rather in the forks of Line creek, now known as the Gipson plantation, with a few other pioneer settlers, viz: Thomas Key, Thomas Eaton Ward, Isom West, Edmond Nunn, _____*

Jacob W. Cobb family portrait in 1884. *Standing left to right*: Robert E. Cobb, William A. Cobb, Thomas M. Cobb, John M. Cobb; *sitting left to right*: Jacob W. Cobb Jr., Mrs. J.W. Cobb Sr., Joseph A. Cobb.

*Dorminy, Hardy Pitman, Thomas Kimmey and a few others not now recollected, made the first settlement this side of Flint river.*

*In the year 1828 Jacob W. Cobb, Avery Wheeler, John W. Cowart, Thomas Key, Edmond Nunn, Isom West, Augustus Nunn and two negroes, Richmond and Judy, his wife, all cropped the Flint river at Shelby's ferry and settled about six miles this side on the waters of Line creek and commenced clearing up the lands just after the Creek Indians had moved across the Chattahoochee river into Alabama. The country was all new except a few little clearings that had been made by the Indians.*

*Game was plentiful and most of the new settlers had to depend upon the woods for their meat. Deer, turkey, o'possum and squirrel were bountiful, notwithstanding the Indians had been in possession of the country for a considerable length of time; they had herds of cattle and raised some corn. The citizens, or early settlers, had no market nearer than Hawkinsville, which was forty-five miles off; their furniture consisted of scaffolds made for beds or bedsteads; they would take one upright piece for a corner post and bore two holes into it and split out a straight piece of timber for rails and stick one end into the post and the other into a hole bored into the logs, and then lay good smooth boards to lie upon. The houses were built with poles, generally of pine or poplar, and covered with boards and weight poles to hold them to their places. The floors were dirt, generally clay, packed down with a mall to make it hard and firm. The chimneys were built of logs to the end of the house.*

*Avery Wheeler started a tanyard on Line creek, and by burning hard wood and making a lye of the ashes, into which he would soak the hides to remove the hair; then he would put the hides into a trough and lay on them a layer of inside bark, then another layer of skins or hides and bark, which he would let stand until the hides were tanned. He would then make shoes out of the hides for the people in the settlement. Soon after that he put up a cooper shop and made such vessels as the people then needed, such as pails, piggins, noggins, a small vessel that would hold from one to three gallons and were used for bath tubs; they were made of red cedar, which was plentiful in the creek swamp at that time, and it never rots.*

*In 1828 the country began to be settled up pretty thick. Lovett B. Smith, William Jordan, who is now living, Ebenezer J. Cottle, Joseph H. Daniel, S. Montgomery, William Pilcher, S. Dozier and W. Reed settled in and around what was known as Pond Town. Jacob Little, William Hughes, Solomon Snelgroves, Peter Faust, Anthony Miller, Allison Culpepper and Leven Adams settled in the western part of the county on Kinchafoonee creek. Jacob Little on Muckalee four miles south of Americus, at which place Little's bridge is now situated.*

*In 1830 Hardy Hay, a man by the name of Dorminy, Elias Hodges, Lamb Hodges, Josiah Suggs and Johnny Suggs settled on what is now known as Philema creek.*

*Much could be written about the characters and customs of people of what was then known as the Tallow Town district, and should I be permitted, sometime in the future I will give some interesting items of that part of the county.*

*Sumter County, Ga., was laid off from Lee county by an act of the legislature in 1831, and the following named persons were chosen to lay off the town: John W. Cowart, Green M. Wheeler, Wright Brady and Jackson Tiner. They selected the lot of land No. 156, in the Twenty-seventh district, on the waters of Muckalee creek and south of Little creek, now known as Town creek. The surveyors pitched their tent near where the Central freight depot now stands. After laying off the streets and court house square, the commissioners met for the purpose of selecting a name for the county site. Each had a name selected and agreed to put all the names in a hat and blindfolded the writer of this article and let the name that I drew out be the one the town should be named, when Lovett B. Smith, one of the commissioners, told the balance of them that he had selected a name that he thought would suit them all, and Americus was the name, which was selected and agreed to by all.*

*The early settlers of the town were Thomas Harvey, Green M. Wheeler, Wright Brady, Jacob W. Cobb, Gid. Thomas, Jackson Tiner, John Tiner, John Kimmey and others. The first house built was a small pine log house built by Pat Brady, on the lot known as the artesian corner. His stock of goods consisted of a barrel of whiskey, a box of tobacco, a box of chalk pipes, keg of powder, lead in bars and a small lot of gun flints. The next house was built by Jacob W. Cobb, on the corner where the tower now stands—Lamar and Lee streets—which was used for a hotel. The first term of the Superior court ever held in this county convened in this building, presided over by Judge Sturgis, of Columbus. The next house was built by Thomas Harvey, on the lot where now stands the McMath store. In 1834 a contract was let to Thomas Gardner to build a courthouse—a two-story wooden building—the lower story for a court room and the upper story for a jury room and for offices for county officials.*

*The first school house built in the town was constructed on Town creek, at the north end of Lee street, just above Elbert Head's fish pond, Thomas Harvey being the first teacher. The first church was built in the old negro cemetery, and the first sermon was preached by Allison Culpepper. The first camp meeting in the county was also at the same place in 1834, conducted by John P. Duncan and John Taley. On the 30th of August, 1834, Robert E. Cobb was born—the first white person born in the town.*

*After the court house was finished the court room was used for church purposes by the Primitives, represented by Allison Culpepper; Methodists, by John Taley; Missionary, by Jonathan Davis; and Universalist, by Rev. Shehan. The first Methodist church was built where the new church is now going up.*

*The first man murdered in the town was one Bozeman, said to have been killed by James Little. The second school taught in the town was at the place opposite W.H.C. Dudley's, on the lot known as the Gibbons Taylor lot, where a big sycamore tree now stands. The writer was going to school there when that tree was set out by the teacher, Horris Dickson.*

*The first lawyer in the town was E.R. Brown. The first doctor in the town was Dr. W.M. Hardwick. The first death occurring in the town was Kinchen Morgan, who died in the year 1835.*

*As this brings me up to the year 1836, I will stop here, and will probably in the future give a history of all the early settlers of the county, together with their customs and peculiarities. I am only writing from memory, and possibly may have made some mistakes.*

Joseph A. Cobb's mother had made her own contribution to local history of the pioneer era when she was interviewed by a *Sumter Republican* reporter at a family reunion in 1884 in East Americus, a neighborhood centered around what is now Mayo and Oglethorpe. It was during this event that the family portrait was taken.

*We then had an interesting conversation with Mrs. Jane Cobb, the mother of the family. Mrs. Cobb is seventy-three years old, remarkably well preserved, possesses a quick, active, sprightly mind, and a most wonderful memory; speaks with freedom and fluency and laughs heartily when she tells of the pranks and practical jokes of the rude pioneers.*

*"My father," said she, "came to what is now Sumter county, January 17th, 1828; on the 9th of the next month my husband and I crossed Flint river and settled on Line creek in the same county, then Lee. My first child was at that time an infant.*

*"We moved to Americus 26th February, 1834. My husband was Clerk of the Superior Court of Lee until Sumter was formed, and then he was Clerk of the Superior Court of this county for a long time. The first Superior Court for Sumter was held at our house; Hon. Grigsby D. Thomas, Judge presiding. The Judge's chair was stationed on a huge goods box and the bar made of goods boxes ranged around the room. After the Judge's charge was over the grand jury marched out of the house and swarmed round a burning heap." Here Mrs. Cobb laughed heartily. "After a while the sheriff borrowed a room and carried them to it.*

*"Holman's, May's, Tiner's and our family were the only families living here in 1834. A man named Moore came here soon afterwards and contracted to build the Court house. He received half his money in advance and left without doing a lick of work.*

*"All the residences here at that time were log houses. Eason Smith had the first framed house built that was ever built in Americus, and Daniel Freeman was the architect; Dr. Hardwick's*

*office was the next framed house. E.R. Brown was the first lawyer here and T.C. Sullivan came soon after. T.B. Harvey, from Jefferson, taught the first school here. Board and lodging for men, women or children was then $7.00 a month. When we came to Americus, the place of the present public square, and from there to the creek, was a dense wilderness, and I have heard in the swamp what was said to be the scream of the panther.*

*"The Tiner boys took the contract for clearing up the square at $90.00. In cutting down a tree they would decide which way they wanted it to fall, and climb up and tie a rope in the top. Then, when the tree was cut nearly enough to fall, a horn was blown and a full turn out of the men in town ran up and pulled the rope. When the trees were all down, the timber and stumps were so thick you could not walk through on the ground."*

*"Mrs. Cobb, how many children have you had and where were they born?"*

*"Fifteen; one born in Wilkinson, three on Line creek, two in Americus and nine at this place, (which was the old family home)* [in East Americus]. *My son Robert E. Cobb was the first boy child ever born in Americus. Eleven of my children are yet living, and seventy-nine of my children and grand, and great grand-children."*

*This is an epitome of the main points, and only the main points of the conversation. Mrs. Cobb promises to give us, in future, a full account of the leading events in the early history of Americus. Her few contemporaries unite in saying there is no one else has so ready a tongue and so accurate a memory as she!*

*Mrs. Cobb is, and has for a great many years, been a pious and consistent member of the Methodist Church, and the high standing, and high respectability and refinement of her family and posterity, prove that she was ever faithful in precept, in example and in all the obligations that duty and affection imposed.*

While Nap Cobb did, indeed, write a number of subsequent articles about Sumter County's pioneer era, his mother unfortunately did not. The Wheeler and Cobb families have numerous descendants still living in our fair community, including yours truly. I will supply a more comprehensive list of those descendants in a future essay.

# The First Family

Happy New Year, one and all! Coincidentally, my arrival for permanent residency in Americus was exactly thirty-one years ago on the first day of that new year (1975). As a college student here, working to complete my bachelor's degree in political science, I learned an early lesson in establishing one's pedigree in a community like ours.

I accompanied my political science professor, Dr. Tommy Williams, to an "Eggs and Issues" breakfast at the Ramada Inn with a cadre of local and state politicos led by Sumter's delegation to the General Assembly, Representative William J. Murray and Senator Hugh Carter. When I was introduced to one of the other politicians, who shall remain nameless since he's still living, he gave me a perfunctory handshake and kind of looked past me, assuming, I suppose, that I was one of those out of town college students. After the question and answer session that ensued, during which I pointed out that my ancestors had been in Americus since before the Civil War, this same politician came over to me and enthusiastically shook my hand and inquired earnestly into my family background. The 180-degree change in his demeanor and attitude was quite astonishing. What a difference it made, establishing my bona fides. I later learned my ancestors here had preceded both Americus's and Sumter County's existence.

In 1999, an intellectually challenged anonymous individual (ever notice how those two characteristics always seem to go together?) in the *Times-Recorder*'s late and, for me, unlamented "Rant and Rave" column amply demonstrated how some of our fellow citizens are so narrow-minded and consumed by their own personal hatreds. This person simplistically assumed that if one is not born or raised and educated here, then that somehow disqualified one from learning enough about local history to become authoritative on the subject. In point of fact, the late Phil Jones told me, at that time, he had lived here all his life and didn't know as much local history as I did. I thanked him for the compliment.

As a longtime bachelor with lots of time on my hands, I had spent ten years carefully scanning every page of nearly every available newspaper ever published in Sumter County, with the lone exception of the Plains's newspaper during Jimmy Carter's presidential administration. Throughout that process, I carefully took notes on all branches of the extended family, as well as anything of historical significance. I augmented that information with literally hundreds, if not thousands, of perusals of public records at both the courthouse and city hall, in addition to annual visits to the state archives, then located in Atlanta. I got to stay there with my Uncle Gilly and Aunt Charlie Purvis for several days each time and it was such a treat.

I caught the genealogy bug about twenty years ago and it's the best hobby I've ever had, although I must confess to spending much of my childhood and adolescence collecting comic books. My mother, bless her heart, kept them stored in her attic, where they remain to this day. Researching and solving puzzles are two of my passions. For example, I thoroughly enjoy the *Atlanta Journal-Constitution*'s daily crossword puzzle, and the Sunday edition also carries the New York and Los Angeles newspapers' super-sized crossword puzzles. It's a great way to unwind and learn at the same time.

My genealogical research received much encouragement and inspiration from my late beloved aunt, Rosalie Purvis Bass, who, throughout her seventy-six years, shared family stories she had grown up with as a lifelong resident of Americus. She learned them by listening to her maternal aunts and uncles, Callie, "Sister," Laurie, "Big" Olin and Oswald, all of whom had vivid memories of the two generations preceding themselves. Every time I found something interesting in the old newspapers, I would take it to Rosalie and she would invariably fill in the background information quite comprehensively. "Sister," by the way, was Nannie Elou Speer, a lifelong spinster who outlived all of her siblings despite a reputation for being sickly. Fortunately, she kept all the family Bible records, photographs and Civil War letters from the Daniel side of the family.

The more I studied my mother's family tree the more I learned about local history. My maternal ancestors were the pioneers of Americus and Sumter County. My great-great-great-great-grandfather, Avery Wheeler, crossed the Flint River at Shelby's Ferry on January 17, 1828, when this area was still the northeastern portion of Lee County. He was on the committee, with his son, Green M. Wheeler and Richard Salter, which determined the site of the county seat for the new Sumter County created on December 26, 1831. When he died on April 25, 1857, he was only the second interment in the newly opened Oak Grove Cemetery. He had been born in Franklin County, North Carolina, on November 23, 1783.

Avery Wheeler's son-in-law, Jacob Wilkins Cobb Sr., my great-great-great-grandfather, crossed the Flint on February 9, 1828, and served as Lee's, then Sumter's, first clerk of superior court. In actuality, the first superior court session was held in his house, Judge Grigsby E. Thomas, presiding. As his wife reminisced some fifty years later, "The Judge's chair was stationed on a huge goods box and the bar made of goods boxes ranged around the room. After the Judge's charge was over the grand jury marched out of the house and swarmed around a burning heap…After a while the sheriff (John Kimmey) borrowed a room and carried them to it." It was J.W. Cobb's desk that was carried off and burned during the farmers' revolt of May 1842. From 1832 to 1837, he served simultaneously as the county ordinary, now probate, judge.

Joseph Absolom "Nap" Cobb
(1829–1914).

On May 13, 1829, Avery Wheeler's son, Benton Moore Wheeler, became the first white person born in what is now Sumter County. The latter's older brother, Green Moore Wheeler, surveyed the original town square in the summer of 1832 and vied with Wright Brady Sr. for the distinction of having built the first house in Americus. G.M. Wheeler served several terms as sheriff (1839–40, 1843, 1846–48, 1850–51) and was the city's first clerk, beginning in 1856. From 1864 until his death on January 17, 1871, he was the county tax collector. His brother, Alexander Watson Wheeler, also was county sheriff (1873–77).

Two of Jacob W. Cobb's sons played historic roles in our fair city. According to his eyewitness account published seven decades after the fact, Joseph Absolom "Nap" Cobb was the three year old who was to draw the name of the new county seat out of a hat in mid-

July 1832, when county treasurer and state Senator Lovett B. Smith proffered the name Americus, "which was selected and agreed to by all." Nap's brother, Robert Emmet Cobb, was the first boy child born in the new courthouse town of Americus on August 28, 1834. When the Cobbs had moved into Americus on February 26 of that year, they, the Holmans, Mays and Tiners were the only families here. Years later, R.E. Cobb would serve several terms on the city council (1867, 1871, 1873–74, 1881–85). During the Civil War, he had been a guard at Camp Sumter, the proper name for what most Americans know as Andersonville Prison.

My great-great-grandmother, Teresa Augusta "Sis" Cobb, married James Alexander Daniel in Americus on June 30, 1859. They were joined in heavenly matrimony by Reverend George Coit, of what is now the First Presbyterian Church. A North Carolina native, James A. Daniel grew up in Milledgeville when it was the state capital. His father, John William Lewis Daniel, was the contractor who built the Baldwin County courthouse in 1838. Through his Lewis line, we are related to Meriwether Lewis, of Lewis and Clark fame. When the Civil War broke out in 1861, J.A. Daniel enlisted in Company K, Ninth Georgia Regiment, the Americus Volunteer Rifles, and fought throughout the war, losing his right leg in one of the battles around Richmond, Virginia, on October 7, 1864. No longer able to be a mechanic or builder, he became a shoemaker until his election as county tax receiver in 1875. He was re-elected twice to that position, until his death in office on July 18, 1887.

My other great-great-grandfather, Amos Coffman Speer, was a native of Morgan County, but grew up in Giles County, Tennessee, and Troup County and Heard County back in his native state. After his marriage in Franklin on March 5, 1850, to Martha Ann Moore, he and his bride moved to Chambers County, Alabama, with his in-laws, before finally locating in Americus in December 1857. In May of 1862, A.C. Speer enlisted in Company K, Fourth Georgia Infantry, the Sumter Light Guards, joining his brother, Moses Speer, who had enlisted the previous year. Serving as an

Private James
Alexander
Daniel, CSA
(1824–1887).

ambulance carrier on the battlefield, Private Amos C. Speer lost
his leg at Fort Steadman, Virginia, on March 25, 1865, as Grant
and Lee were hurtling toward Appomattox Courthouse. For several years after the war, he could be seen plowing his fields on the
wooden leg carved by his uncle, Thomas Dixon Speer, our state
representative in 1865–66.

Amos C. Speer spent almost all of his remaining years in public
office as tax collector (1871–79), ordinary judge (1885–1900) and
treasurer (1903–07). He died October 19, 1908, and is buried with
his first wife, his son Everett and two grandchildren, Mattie and
Lawson Schneider, in the family cemetery near the old Simpson
place, which had been built of yellow heart pine timber during
the war by Thomas D. Speer's thirty-nine slaves. Thieves stole the
belts from his steam sawmill in 1862, which explains the unfinished

lumber in one of the home's original rooms. T.D. Speer sold what was left of the two thousand-acre plantation to Thomas Simpson in 1874 and moved to Norcross, Georgia, "to get away from cotton fields and negroes," as he delicately phrased it in a letter to his brother the following year. His racial attitude is a little confusing to me as his cook, Elvy, who had been owned by him in Morgan County and moved with him to Sumter in 1853, took his surname after emancipation and resided nearby in the 1870 census, with her family, sons Isaac and Aaron, and daughters Adeline, Lavinia and Susan.

When James and Teresa Daniel's daughter, Sarah Jane "Jennie" Daniel, married Amos and Martha Ann Speer's son, William Henry, on January 20, 1878, in Americus, their youngest daughter, Rosalie Speer, would grow up to be my maternal grandmother. She married Edgar May Purvis, formerly of Taylor County, on March 28, 1906, at the family home on Cherry Street, where First State Bank is currently located. She was fourteen and he was twenty-three. Their youngest child, Edna May, born at home on South Hampton Street on March 4, 1928, was my mother.

My sister Mary Jo Anderson's boys, Matthew Alexander "Alec" and Mark Edward "Chip" Simmons Jr., are the eighth generation of my family to live in Sumter County. Other bloodline descendants of Avery Wheeler still residing here include my cousins Frank L. Purvis and Carroll E. "Tump" Purvis, and the latter's daughters, Teresa Carol (Mrs. Keith Teasley) and her children, Hope Elizabeth and Hannah Grace, Sheryl Denise (Mrs. B.T. Rush III) and her children, Robert Tucker and Mary Nell; John L. Purvis; Mrs. Randolph B. Jones Sr. (formerly Rufulyn "Biddy" Mathews), and her son, Randy Jr., and his daughter, Nancy Stallings; Miss Nan Gunn; J.T. Bass Jr.; Saranne (Mrs. Bobby) Peacock and her sons, Hugh and Patrick, and the latter's daughter, Emily; W.C. Sullivan IV, and his daughter, Shelly, who, coincidentally, works at Citizens Bank of Americus, whose president, Rick Whaley, is also a descendant, along with his mother, Mrs. Cordelia Horne Whaley, and his brother Rusty, and the latter's two children, Jimmy and Ashton; Mrs. Georgia Scott and her children, Layton and Ansley; and, last but not least, Jim Speer, who, with his wife Lillian, returned to Americus in 1999 and, like your humble author, have become permanent residents.

Are we proud of our ancestors' contributions to Sumter County and Americus? You ain't just whistling Dixie!

# Various Visitors

In twenty-six years of teaching, I have often heard my students express negative opinions about our fair community. Usually the complaint is to the effect that this place is boring because nothing ever happens here. Unfortunately for them, in their youth the vast majority of them lack any historic perspective. It is my great desire that my discerning adult readers will share this material with their younger counterparts.

Americus and Sumter County have hosted heads of state, international personalities, major historical figures, prominent national politicians, Hollywood celebrities, military heroes and even notorious artifacts.

After his defeat for re-election, native son Jimmy Carter was visited at his Plains home by Egyptian President Anwar Sadat in August 1981, just two months before the latter's assassination. The month after Sadat's courtesy call, Israeli Prime Minister Menachem Begin followed suit. Both men paid homage to the former president's crucial role in his greatest achievement in office, peace between Egypt and Israel through the Camp David Accords. Sixteen years later, for much the same reason, Palestinian Authority President Yasser Arafat came to Plains in March 1997.

Other internationally famous individuals included the first European to venture through this territory. According to legend, Spanish explorer Hernando DeSoto, discoverer of the Mississippi River, encamped on the site of the community that bears his name in March 1540. Older residents there can locate the well supposed to have been dug by DeSoto's men.

Probably the most well known international visitor was a complete unknown during his two-week stay in May 1923. A wing-walking daredevil, he made his first solo flight at Souther Field and bought a $500 "Jenny" from John Alden Wyche. Almost exactly four years later, Charles A. Lindbergh would stun the world with his solo transatlantic flight to Paris.

Major historical figures with business to conduct here involved two sessions of the Georgia Supreme Court. Our first courthouse hosted that esteemed panel, consisting of Joseph Henry Lumpkin, Hiram Warner and Eugenius A. Nisbet, in July 1847. Exactly seven years later, in our then new antebellum brick courthouse, J.H. Lumpkin, Henry L. Benning and Ebenezer A. Starnes presided over the court's final session in Americus.

After the Civil War the Reconstruction era got underway in Americus with the arrival in August 1865 of the 147th Regiment, Illinois Volunteers, U.S. Army, commanded by Colonel H.F. Sickles. Since General Howell Cobb's family had resided there during the war's final year, his mansion at the northeast corner of College and Lee became federal headquarters. Built by Willis A. Hawkins circa 1855, for the rest of that century it was the home of railroad president Samuel H. Hawkins. For much of the next century it was occupied by Dr. W.S. Prather and finally razed by his daughter in September 1963.

Georgia's preeminent poet, Sidney Lanier, gave the commence-ment speech at the Furlow Masonic Female College graduation of June 1869. In a similar vein, but to a vastly different audience, Booker T. Washington spoke at the Americus Institute at the invitation of its president, Professor Major W. Reddick, in May 1908. The former educational edifice was located at the site on South Jackson of the old Furlow Grammar School (only the original cornerstone remains). The latter existed as a seventeen-acre complex from 1897 to 1932, at the present site of A.S. Staley Middle School on North Lee.

Leading lights of the late Confederacy were frequent visitors. Governor Joseph E. Brown made a speech in Americus in January 1864. General Joseph E. Johnston visited the Methodist Church in December 1868, much to the delight of the congregants. Robert Toombs, the "Unreconstructed Rebel," made a fiery speech at the courthouse in November 1873. His best friend, Confederate States of America (CSA) vice-president Alexander H. Stephens, was the commencement speaker at the aforementioned Furlow Masonic Female College in June 1875 and returned to Americus as governor in September 1882 shortly before his death. General John B. Gordon made a gubernatorial campaign swing through here in May 1886 and came for an exhibition of reminiscences at Glover's Opera House in February 1900. CSA President Jefferson Davis's train stopped at the Central Depot in November 1887, his frail health allowing only a brief appearance.

A Confederate veteran and noted Georgia humorist, the Lewis Grizzard of the nineteenth century, Bill Arp made a presentation at the Jackson Street School auditorium in October 1880. In August 1889, Henry W. Grady, the voice of the "New South," spoke at the Confederate veterans' reunion at the courthouse. Eminent historian Lucien Lamar Knight addressed the Confederate Memorial Day ceremony at Oak Grove Cemetery in April 1899.

Discounting the flood of vice-presidential aspirants in 1976, many prominent national politicians have graced our presence on an individual basis. In June 1893, Congressman William Jennings Bryan had dinner with Speaker Charles F. Crisp at that worthy gentleman's new home on Taylor. During one of his three unsuccessful attempts as the Democratic presidential candidate, Bryan made a whistle-stop campaign speech at the Central Depot en route to Columbus in February 1900. Bryan came back in June 1919 at First Baptist Church to promote the League of Nations and the anti-saloon league.

During the 1912 presidential election, Democrat Woodrow Wilson made a whistle-stop speech at the Central Depot in April of that year. Later, his vice-president, Thomas Riley Marshall, probably more famous for his quote, "What this country needs is a good five cent cigar," spoke from the Windsor balcony to the Woodmen of the World convention in March 1917.

Another successful Democratic presidential candidate, soon-to-be-New York Governor Franklin D. Roosevelt, spoke to the Chamber of Commerce in the Windsor dining hall in February 1928. Spending that night at the Windsor, he returned to Warm Springs the next day. In May 1964, Alabama Governor George C. Wallace made a race-baiting speech at the Country Club in his initial foray into presidential politics. Lester Maddox, who would make it to the governor's mansion a year later, led a six hundred-person Ku Klux Klan march through downtown Americus in August 1965. From the opposite end of the political spectrum, Reverend Jesse Jackson appeared in Americus twice in the presidential campaigns of 1984 and 1988. As another guest of the Windsor Hotel, his most recent visit was a speech at Bethesda Baptist Church in April 2001.

Besides President Carter's, cabinet officials have shown up in more than one instance. In April 1960, Secretary of Agriculture Ezra Taft Benson toured the Mormons' Deseret Farms in the fifteenth district. Orville Freeman, who held the same post for L.B.J., led a campaign rally at the ballpark on Bell and Oak in October 1964. The second Secretary of Health, Education and Welfare, Marion B. Folsom, visited his wife's sisters in Americus in April 1963. Former Secretary of State Dean Rusk was the keynote speaker at the inauguration of Dr. William Capitan at Georgia Southwestern in May 1980. Secretary of the Army Togo D. West Jr. was the featured speaker at Memorial Day ceremonies at Andersonville in May 1997. The executive branch was represented one more time in May 1996 when NASA administrator Dan Goldin and astronaut Kenneth Bowersox attended a forum at South Georgia Technical College's Griffin Bell Aerospace Center.

The entertainment world has been well represented along these lines. Actress Laura Keene, who performed in *Our American Cousin* at President Abraham Lincoln's assassination, presented the play at the Americus city hall, at the northeast corner of Cotton and Lamar, in December 1870. John Phillip Sousa, the "March King," was trapshooting as a guest of the Americus Country Club in April 1913. Sarah Bernhardt performed in a five-act play at Dudley's Opera House in March 1916. During a national flying tour in October 1929, Gary Cooper literally "dropped in" at Souther Field for a few hours. Earl "Fatha" Hines and his orchestra played at the Rylander's scrip dance in September 1936. Western actor Dan Duryea visited the Martin Theater while on a promotional tour in October 1951. The soon to be Wonder Woman, Lynda Carter, did precisely the same in February 1976. Movie and television star Martin Sheen, a Civil War buff, visited Andersonville and stayed at the Windsor in March 2006.

Michael Rennie, British star of the sci-fi classic *The Day the Earth Stood Still*, trained as a Royal Air Force (RAF) pilot at Souther Field during World War II. One of the original "Dead End Kids," Don Latorre, was an army recruiter in Americus in September 1957. Researching the Andersonville prison for a Columbia Studios movie, Pulitzer Prize-winning author MacKinlay Kantor and actor/folksinger Burl Ives toured the facility in June 1958. Another Pulitzer winner, Robert Penn Warren, spoke at what is now Georgia Southwestern State University in February 1966.

Miscellaneous professional speakers were invited by various local organizations. Radio commentator Paul Harvey addressed the Chamber of Commerce in January 1969. Dr. Norman Vincent Peale did likewise in February 1974. CBS newsman Roger Mudd participated in a Georgia Southwestern lyceum in January 1970.

Paul Anderson, the "World's Strongest Man," made inspirational speeches at the Americus Kiwanis Club in April 1963, Lee Street Methodist Church in November 1965, Leslie United Methodist Church in July 1971 and the Americus Rotary Club in April 1973. He holds the personal appearance record.

"Shoeless" Joe Jackson coached and played at the Barlow Ballpark in Americus in the summer of 1923.

Other celebrities over the years included three Miss Americas. In July 1953, Macon native Neva Jane Langley was guest of honor at the "Manufacturers' Day" parade in Americus. Debbye Turner was at Belk's Department Store on a promotional tour in April 1990. Kimberly Aiken worked on Habitat for Humanity's 30,000[th] house in June 1994.

Personal visits were recorded for Jimmy Stewart and his wife, who ate at Carter's Fried Chicken while en route to a Sea Island golf course in October 1973. Johnny Cash and his wife, June Carter, toured Plains in March 1975. Gary Merrill paid a house call on his friends, Leonard and Marie Waitsman, in July 1976, as well as on several other occasions. ABC's "Carter Country" star, Victor French, came to Plains in November 1977 to soak up a little local color.

Performances here included the Jaycee sponsored Roy Orbison concert at Americus High School in November 1966. The Four Seasons gave a concert at Georgia Southwestern in April 1969. Soprano Mattiwilda Dobbs sang at the Georgia Southwestern Black History program in February 1975. At the Rylander's grand re-opening in October 1999, Lynn Anderson, Pat Boone, the Indigo Girls and the McGuire Sisters all made appearances.

Nationally televised programs have originated in Sumter County as well. In May 1980, NBC's "Real People" filmed the "Many Pauses" bowling team of Zine Bendimire, Mary Crawford, Joan Melton and Evelyn Wages. Hume Cronyn, his wife Jessica Tandy and Esther Rolle filmed "To Dance With the White Dog" in and around Sumter City, while guests of the Windsor in August 1993. In November 1998, CBS's Dan Rather interviewed locals for a "60 Minutes II" story on the Daniel Colwell case. Although not a national broadcaster at the time, NBC's Tom Brokaw interviewed locals during the civil rights demonstrations in July and August 1965 as a reporter for WSB-TV in Atlanta.

From the world of sports came former heavyweight boxing champion John L. Sullivan, performing in the play *The Man From Boston* at Glover's Opera House in April 1893. Two of Major

League baseball's greatest stars had Americus connections. In April 1922, Ty Cobb and the Detroit Tigers played the Americus team at the old Barlow ballpark near the swimming pool. Cobb returned as the guest of his relative and my friend, Preston Cobb, at the Americus Rotary Club in June 1956. On that same field in July and August of 1923, "Shoeless" Joe Jackson was captain of the Americus team, putting on homerun exhibitions with his bat, "Black Betsy." Sportswriter Grantland Rice and cartoonist Rube Goldberg paid a call on the former's mother-in-law, Mrs. Florence D. Hollis, at her home on Taylor in January 1934.

Two military heroes of World War I came to Americus. Sergeant Alvin C. York gave a patriotic speech at the Rylander in June 1921. Captain Eddie Rickenbacker, then president of Eastern Airlines, inspected the Municipal Airport, south of Columbia, in June 1938. Vietnam War hero and POW Senator John McCain gave the key-note speech at the dedication of the National POW Museum at Andersonville National Historic Site in April 1998.

In February 1896, socialist labor leader Eugene V. Debs gave a speech at city hall. United Mine Workers president John L. Lewis gassed up his car at the Lighthouse in January 1947, when it was still situated between the Forsyth and Lamar viaducts.

Temperance crusader Carrie Nation appeared in *Ten Nights in a Bar Room* at Dudley's Opera House in October 1907. Other social reformers doing time in Sumter County included Dr. Martin Luther King Jr., who was a guest of Sheriff Fred D. Chappell at the courthouse jail in December 1961. Dr. King's father would be the featured speaker at Georgia Southwestern's Black History program in February 1976. Comedian turned civil rights activist Dick Gregory led a voter registration drive at the courthouse in August 1965. State Representative Julian Bond spoke at Georgia Southwestern in May 1974.

We have also been visited by somewhat notorious artifacts. In June 1936, Bonnie and Clyde's death car was exhibited at the Americus Auto Company. A Japanese two-man submarine captured at Pearl Harbor was on display across from the Windsor in

March 1944. Adolf Hitler's personal limousine was parked opposite the Martin Theater in November 1951. Although technically not an artifact, Japanese Emperor Hirohito's white stallion paid us a visit in January 1952. On a more positive note, the Centennial Olympic Torch was carried by locals through Sumter County in July 1996.

Finally, let me put to rest some apocryphal claims about gangsters. It is true that "Scarface" Al Capone was spotted by a *Times-Recorder* reporter on a train at the Central Depot in April 1930, en route from Chicago to Miami. Floyd Lowery's claim that John Dillinger was a guest of the Windsor is belied by the fact that when he was killed by the FBI, no mention was made in the local media and if there had been a connection I assure you it would have been cited.

For you who may have regarded this as some sleepy backwater where nothing ever happens, I hope this effort has disabused you of such notions.

# The Fourth Estate

Although Americus was established in 1832, the town did not get its first local newspaper until twenty-two years later. At the behest of Charles J. Malone and other prominent antebellum citizens, Charles W. Hancock, a South Carolina native who published and edited a newspaper in Washington, Georgia, was persuaded to relocate here. C.J. Malone, who had moved a house to Americus from Oglethorpe after the yellow fever epidemic there, situated it on a large lot at the southwest corner of Starkville Road and Hill Street. The former is now Lee Street and the latter is now College Street. At the back end of the lot, Malone moved or built a house for the new editor as an incentive to come here. That house is now on the southwest corner of College and Hancock and now you know how the latter street got its name. It changed from an avenue to a drive in July 1941.

The first issue of C.W. Hancock's *Sumter Republican* was dated February 23, 1854. A staunch Democrat, he named it for our form of government, although, ironically, the Republican Party was born in Ripon, Wisconsin, only five days later. Editor Hancock, a man of strong opinion, was physically attacked twice for his commentaries. In 1857 he was in a shootout on the courthouse square in which his antagonist, Harvey W. Shaw, was killed. Shaw's deadly ambush was a reaction to Hancock's published criticism of the former's involvement in the death of a visiting doctor. In 1871 Charles W. Hancock was brutally beaten by the city marshal, Stephen H. Mitchell, who had taken offense at the editor's observations about his lack of child-rearing skills.

On June 14, 1854, the *Southwestern News*, Democratic in politics, became the *Republican's* first in a series of challengers. Initiated by J.T. and J.L.D. Register, it was subsequently owned by William B. Guerry, Esquire, followed by Reverend Adam A. Robinson. During its last two years, 1861–62, under A.B. Seals, its name was changed to the *Americus Weekly Post*.

Americus's earliest extant city directory in August 1869 listed Hancock's *Republican*, which then came out weekly and tri-weekly, along with E. and J.R. Christian's *Americus Courier*, also a weekly and tri-weekly. The editor's wife was a teacher at the Freedmen's School at the corner of Forsyth and Prince.

May of 1879 was the beginning of the end for the city's oldest newspaper. The *Americus Recorder* debuted with Merrell Callaway and the return of J.R. Christian. They were succeeded more successfully by a Yankee transplant, Major William L. Glessner, editor and publisher, with his son-in-law Henry C. Storey as local editor. In 1890 they built the residence at the southeast corner of Glessner and Lee, hence the street name. Their keen competition doomed the *Sumter Republican*, which came to an ignominious end in 1889.

Meanwhile, in the black community, Professor George Washington Franklin Phillips, first principal of the McCay Hill School, edited and published the *Americus Monitor* beginning August 1, 1886. Another weekly black newspaper, the *Americus Tribune*, began circulation November 3, 1891. During 1911, W. Robert Mack edited and published the *Americus Chronicle*. No readable copies of these exist, unfortunately. Actually, the time capsule in the cornerstone of the Victorian era courthouse includes a copy of the *Americus Monitor*, but it was too badly decayed to be read when it was opened in 1960. The torch is currently being carried by Dr. John D. Marshall, publisher, whose monthly *AmericUSumter Observer* made its appearance in February 1997.

Americus newspaper banners from the *Sumter Republican* through the *Americus Times-Recorder*.

The boom year of 1890 saw the beginning of construction of the Windsor Hotel as well as two newcomers to the field of journalistic endeavor. On January 17, 1890 the *Daily Americus Times*, financed by a local syndicate, took on the *Recorder* head to head. The directors, James Fricker, Merrell Callaway, John R. Shaw, Arthur Rylander, Daniel F. Davenport, Dr. James B. Hinkle, George

D. Wheatley, Charles M. Wheatley, Henry C. Bagley, Dr. Willis P. Burt, Moses Speer, Noah G. Prince and John A. McDonald, read like a list of who's who in Americus and Sumter County. The *Times* was edited by R.H. Brumby, with James W. Furlow, of one of the city's most eminent families, as city editor. On April 25, 1890 the *Americus Evening Herald* began its more than ten-year history (I have a special edition from Easter 1901).

Even though Americus was Georgia's eighth largest city at the time, it could not financially sustain three newspapers. At the end of February 1891, both the *Times* and *Recorder* ceased publication and consolidated into the *Times-Recorder* under Captain Bascom Myrick, resuming circulation with the April 8, 1891 edition. That worthy gentleman's untimely death in 1895 led to Americus having the only journal in Georgia owned, published and edited with a woman at the helm!

Marie Louise Scudder Myrick single-handedly ran the *Times-Recorder* until her retirement in 1907. Briefly, beginning November 3, 1901, despite her decidedly racist views, which she expressed frequently on the printed page, the *Times-Recorder* began a weekly "Column for Colored People" by Dr. E.J. Brinson. He, too, has a street named for him. Such a special feature would not reappear until Mrs. Ann Witcher's edited "News of Local Negro Community" from September 1967 until May 1971. During Mrs. Myrick's tenure, she outlasted the *Herald*, the *Penny Press* of the mid-1890s and the 1902–03 *Americus Daily Press*. Concurrent with her departure, H.P. Trimble began the *Americus Evening News*, but it only lasted two months from February through March 1907.

For the next five years the *Times-Recorder* was owned by Thomas Gamble, formerly of Savannah, who returned to that city in 1912 and later became its mayor. Two of the editors employed by new owner George R. Ellis, formerly of Lumpkin, led to some changes. Franc Mangum was elected the first president of the Americus Rotary Club in September 1918 but left the next month to enlist for World War I. His successor, Quimby Melton, switched the

*Times-Recorder* to an afternoon paper to facilitate his courtship of Postmaster D.F. Davenport's daughter in 1919.

From November 1911 through February 1917, the *Times-Recorder*'s only competition came from the weekly (later daily) *South Georgia Progress*, Clarence A. Ames, managing editor. A complete set of the *Daily Press* and *South Georgia Progress* survived the ravages of time and may be found on microfilm at the Lake Blackshear Regional Library's Special Collections Room.

On January 1, 1931, the *Times-Recorder*'s latest owner, William Prescott Allen, sold it to a Midwest syndicate, which sent James R. Blair of Indiana to Americus to be its new editor. Five years later he bought out the syndicate's interest and, for about a half-century, he and his son, William E. Blair, made the newspaper a family affair.

The *Times-Recorder*'s last major rival before the modern era was E.L. Gammage's weekly *Tri-County News*, which serviced Sumter, Schley and Webster. Original editor Harry P. Leadingham was followed by Lovelace Eve who had come over from the *Times-Recorder*. It joined the news fray early in October 1933 and ceased publication, under different ownership, about 1953. Many of those issues are also on microfilm at the library. During the summer of 1941, Buddy Pilcher edited his own daily, the *Americus News*.

J. Frank Myers's *Sumter Free Press*, edited by Don Fletcher, a weekly that began with a free edition on March 11, 1998, was subsequently acquired by William H. McGowan and William J. Murray, its present proprietors. Editor Fletcher left the *Free Press* to launch Thomas Holloway's *Sumter News* in November 2001. For four years with both papers, I thoroughly enjoyed writing about local history with brother Fletcher, who has since left the profession.

# The Man Who Made Americus

Timothy Mathews Furlow was born on October 1, 1814, in or near Madison, Georgia, a son of Charles and Margaret Mathews Furlow. His mother's demise only two years later sent young Tim to Bibb County to be raised by his uncle and namesake. Timothy Mathews had represented that county as its state senator in 1825–26, setting a pattern of public service that his nephew would emulate in later years.

T.M. Furlow received his first education in Twiggs County but he mostly grew up in the Clinton community outside Macon. After graduating from what is now the University of Georgia, he returned to Clinton and married Miss Charlotte Mary Lowther on November 5, 1835. Two children blessed this union, William Lowther and Charlotte Mary Lowther Furlow. Unfortunately, both his wife and baby daughter died only three years later, the former in childbirth on July 19, 1838, and the latter, just shy of three months in age, on October 13. The son, Captain W.L. Furlow, would later be killed in the Civil War at the battle of McDowell, Virginia on May 8, 1862.

On November 3, 1839, Timothy M. Furlow married his second wife, Miss Margaret Ella, second daughter of Major Tarpley Holt, of Bibb County. Their children were Charles Timothy, Nellie (Mrs.

James Callaway), Kate (Mrs. Merrell Callaway) and Hallie (Mrs. A.D. Gatewood).

With the arrival of the 1840s, T.M. Furlow began a sojourn into the world of politics that, off and on, would last until the end of his life a half century later. In 1841 he represented Bibb in the state house, followed the next year by a turn in the state senate. On January 19, 1861, he and Sumter's two other delegates, Willis A. Hawkins and Henry Davenport Jr., voted for Georgia's Ordinance of Secession at Milledgeville, then the state capital. In 1863, Timothy M. Furlow ran unsuccessfully for governor, coming in third in a three-man race. As in Bibb, he represented Sumter as our senator from 1861–63 and representative from 1875–76. He also served as mayor of Americus for the years 1866–68 and 1871. When he died in 1890, he was just completing his first term as Sumter's tax collector and had been re-nominated to a second one.

Moving from Bibb to near Perry, Georgia, in 1845, after a brief hiatus from politics there, Timothy M. Furlow relocated to the village of Americus in November 1849. The next year's federal census recorded a white population of just 308. As a Democrat, a Methodist and a Mason, he found himself quite at home in our antebellum community. A longtime steward of what is now First United Methodist Church, T.M. Furlow served on the building committee and donated liberally to the construction of that denomination's antebellum sanctuary in April 1856 on their current site. It replaced their original 1845 structure across the street where Sumter Bank & Trust's drive-in is presently situated.

As a Mason and strong proponent of education, Timothy M. Furlow was on the board that incorporated the Americus Female Institute in June 1852. It was administered by Reverend Phillip A. Strobel, who wrote the seminal work on Georgia's Salzburgers, and was located at the northeast corner of Brown and Taylor. Reverend Strobel resided across the street in an earlier version of what is known today as the old Lanier home.

Furlow Lawn in 1885.

This effort for equal opportunity education unfortunately failed after a couple of years and T.M. Furlow, Allen S. Cutts and Willis A. Hawkins spearheaded and substantially financed the construction, along with Masonic Lodge 13, of the Furlow Masonic Female College, which opened in June 1859 on the site of the old Furlow Grammar School at the northwest corner of College and Jackson. This structure was used as the city's first public school in 1880 but was replaced by the current building in 1914. T.M. Furlow served on the first Americus city school board in 1873, as he had done two years earlier with the county school board.

Shortly after his arrival, as well as that of his brother, James W. Furlow, Timothy M. Furlow bought a forty-acre tract of land bounded now by College, Elm, Hill and Lee, and it was known as "the Lawn" for the rest of the century. J.W. Furlow acquired the large tract, diagonally across Lee (then the Starkville Road) from his brother, where the former Mary Shayne home is located. T.M. Furlow's property was elegantly landscaped and populated with tame deer, myriad shrubs and trees and gravel walkways. The churches used the Lawn for their annual picnics. As a matter of fact, Central Baptist Church, from 1897 to 1917, was named Furlow Lawn Baptist Church because of its location on the northwest corner.

The developers of what was then the South Western Railroad had reached Oglethorpe in 1851 but intended to move west to Pond Town, now better known as Ellaville. Timothy M. Furlow approached the railroad's directors, determined the necessary financing to change the route to Americus and within a few weeks raised the $75,000 subscription. He specifically cited the help of William W. Barlow, Wright Brady, Edmund R. Brown, George M. Dudley, Augustus H. Gibson, Joseph J. Granberry, Jesse Hardy, Robert C. Jenkins, Newnan McBain and H. Kent McCay. Five of these worthy gentlemen have roads or streets named after them.

The first railroad engine pulled into Americus on October 1, 1854, and by the end of the decade the town's population increased over tenfold from the decade's beginning! In one of a series of articles he wrote for the *Americus Recorder* from September to December 1886, entitled "Ancient Americus," Timothy M. Furlow explained the economic benefits of railroads to a cotton-producing center such as existed here. The city's subsequent growth to become the eighth largest in the state by 1890 simply proved his point.

Bereft of his considerable fortune after the Civil War, T.M. Furlow joined with his brother in the mercantile business at the head of Cotton Avenue. In 1875 he sold to J.W. Furlow his beloved Lawn estate and to Samuel H. Hawkins, about the same time, his plantation of several thousand acres encompassing the present site of DeSoto and its environs. Barlow and Furlow streets were cut through the Lawn in 1883 and the subdivision was developed mostly by S.H. Hawkins. T.M. Furlow's mansion was substantially altered, one wing moved to his brother's property, an additional floor added to the original, then moved to face east on Barlow. There, in 1905, it became the city's first hospital until 1914, after which it briefly served as a business school. It was partially demolished in July 1935, the upper floor being converted into a nondescript duplex, which, coincidentally, I lived in as a six year old in 1957.

Upon his sudden death during an operation for mouth cancer in Atlanta on December 2, 1890, Timothy Mathews Furlow was universally mourned by the people of Americus and Sumter

County and laid to his eternal rest in Oak Grove Cemetery. Some of his numerous descendants remain in the city for which he worked so hard to help reach its potential.

# From Slave to Capitalist, Philanthropist and Republican Party Leader

The gentleman whose portrait adorns this article is, in my opinion, one of the most remarkable individuals in local history. From the base status of slave to the equivalent of a modern-day multimillionaire, Elbert Head was truly the self-made man. His life and contributions to our community make him an example any people would do well to emulate.

I can do no better than his own words from an interview republished in the *Americus Recorder* of November 17, 1889. This autobiography originally appeared in the *AME Church Review*, Volume VI.

> *I was born in Wilkes county, Georgia, September 7, 1817, and belonged to a man by the name of William Colbert. He also owned my mother, whose name was Dollie. She had three children, two girls—one named Jane and the other Lucinda. My father was taken away before I could recollect, and all my kindred are now dead.*
>
> *When about five years old I was carried from Wilkes to Elbert county, where my mother was sold and carried to parts unknown to me. I was then taken from Georgia to Shelby county, West Tennessee, not far from Memphis. There I remained until I was about fifteen years old, when I was carried to Dallas county,*

Portrait of Elbert Head (1817–1892).

*Alabama, near Cohobby where I remained two years. I was taken back to Georgia and settled about four miles from Forsyth, Monroe county. In 1836 I helped to build a steam mill, the first mill that sawed a stick of lumber for the Monroe Railroad which ran from Macon to Forsyth. I worked under a man by the name of Bob Findley, who came there from Philadelphia, Pennsylvania. After that I worked on a farm for a good many years.*

*In 1840 I married a woman by the name of Harriet Head, who belonged to B.J. Head, and who bought me after the death of my first owner, and we lived as man and wife a little over forty years. Since her death, April 28, 1883, I have lived single.*

*I served William Colbert until August 8, 1842, when he died. The same fall I was carried to the court house in Forsyth, Georgia, and was sold to the highest bidder. A man by the name of*

# From Slave to Capitalist, Philanthropist and Republican Party Leader

*B.J. Head bought me, which was my desire. He and I got along pleasantly, without any difficulties; we both could trust each other. I attended to his business and run his farm until 1851, when he allowed me to hire my time. I hired myself and wife from that time until June 1, 1865. At that time we were all set free.*

*I came to Americus on January 22, 1854, after living in several other places in Georgia, and have remained here ever since. I have seen the small village grow to what it is now. As a slave I was successful, being blessed with more privileges than the common run of slaves at that time.*

*On the first day of June 1865, I was set free in this county. At that time I was keeping a public washing and ironing establishment, but I laid it down from that time. I felt a great joy that we were free, but it made me feel sad to think that there was a whole nation of us set free and none with homes. There were several days that I shed tears on account of our homeless conditions, but I fixed my course and set my stakes to deal in real estate, and I feel that I have been successful and that the Lord has blessed my efforts. I feel that I shall serve Him the balance of my days. I thank Him for my success.*

*I have built since freedom eighty-seven houses in Americus, and have sold one hundred and sixteen vacant lots to both white and colored people. I have experimented in fish raising for twenty years, and have had four ponds. A great many have asked me about my success in raising fish, and I will take pleasure in telling anyone what I know about it. I find in raising fish the size will be according to the depth of your water. I had three small ponds and a large one. In the large pond, where it afforded water ten or twelve feet deep, there was always plenty of big fish.*

*In 1868 I joined the AME Church, and I have tried to live in its faith ever since. I have had the honor of being elected five times to the National Convention to help nominate the Presidents. My people have conferred more honors upon me than I ever could have expected.*

Head's Bottom on North Lee Street in 1885

Elbert Head's precise memory for dates and places and his keen business acumen strongly evidenced his intellectual attainments. Despite living in a society ruled by white supremacy, he was a philanthropist, capitalist, political leader, devout Christian and devoted family man.

Allow me to elaborate. As a philanthropist, Elbert Head financed the education of scores of young people and guaranteed the bonds of those he deemed worthy. Head's Academy, at Scott's Mater Tabernacle on South Hampton, was praised in the *Sumter Republican* of July 8, 1870. It continued providing a quality education for a dozen more years. In January 1871, under the Public School Law, Americus commissioners and trustees elected were T.M. Furlow, Peter F. Brown, Dr. G.F. Cooper and Elbert Head. When the city schools began operating in January 1880, following a seven-year court battle, black students attended either Bethesda Baptist on South Forrest or Elbert Head's two-story building at the northeast corner of Forsyth and Poplar.

As he stated in his autobiographical interview, there was ample reason to list Elbert Head's occupation in the 1880 federal census as capitalist (in 1870 he was a broker). He owned almost all of the two blocks bounded by Bay, Jackson, Lee and where Prince is now. He also had extensive holdings on Ashby, Forsyth, Poplar and Winn, as well as McCay Hill. Elbert Head's four fishponds were located in what was then called Head's Bottom, at Ashby and Lee. Alderman R.E. Cobb jokingly described Head's pond as having 4.5 million trout, 45 inches long, with cat and bream between each and that Head had to haul water to cover the fish! He and his wife Harriet ran public bathhouses and a swimming pool there, on the east side of Lee, during the 1870s and 1880s. He definitely believed in diversification.

Elbert Head was the Republican Party leader of this congressional district for almost three decades after emancipation. As he noted, he attended the national conventions, including having a medal pinned on him by President Ulysses S. Grant in 1872. He ran unsuccessfully for the legislature in November 1870, with two whites, J.R. Simmons and Joseph Mulholland. Editor C.W. Hancock snidely commented that "Morally, the negro is the best." All political meetings in the black community were held at Liberty Hall, a substantial two-story frame structure, which had been built by Elbert Head on the west side of Lee, halfway between Ashby and J.R. Campbell Sr. (formerly Wild). He was held in such esteem by both races that he and James Ellis, in August 1883, were chosen as the first black jurors to serve in the history of Sumter County.

We are fortunate, indeed, that we have a verbatim interview of Elbert Head by the *Times-Recorder* on June 16, 1892. The reporter recorded his comments preserving the thick dialect spoken at the time.

> *Elbert Head is back from Minneapolis where he has been attend-*
> *ing the Republican convention. Since his return he has been*
> *surrounded by the negroes and has told them over and over again*
> *how the convention did its work. He is one of the wealthiest*
> *negroes in the state, and besides that is an old antebellum darkey,*

*who is popular with the white folks.* To the Times-Recorder *Head talked a good deal about the convention.*

*"Your man got beat, didn't he?" he was asked.*

*"No, sah; certainly not. Mr. Harrison was nominated and dat's de man I wanted."*

*"When you went to the convention in '88 you were for Blaine, weren't you?"*

*"I didn't say, sah, who I wuz fer. Dere was a contestin' delegation ef you remember, and when axed I stated dat I couldn't say before I wuz admitted who I would vote for."*

*He says the convention was one of the best he has attended, and this made the eighth time he was present and saw a Republican nominated for president...*

*About Blaine he had this to say:*

*"You're a paper man, an' I musn't say too much, but you know dat Mrs. Blaine belongs to a certain society, and it's presumed dat he would lean that way. I reckon he's about de smartest man in the country, but you see 'bout dat society."*

*"What society do you mean?"*

*"Wal, you is a paper man, an' I musn't say much. You know dere is lots of Catholics in this country, an' de Sisters uv charity cum around an' wait on you, an' dey is sweet and kind an' everybody luvs um, an' it won't be more'n 100 years before dey hab control uv de whole United States."*

*That's about as near an explanation of the society idea he spoke of that he would make to a "paper man."*

*"How about the buying of southern delegates?"*

*"Wal, sah, ef sich an effort wuz made, I doan' know it, and I certainly would know it ef anybody did. I am sho' Georgia didn't sell, an' I doan think any unfair means were taken by either the Harrison men or the Blaine men. No, sah, dere wuz no buyin' an' no sellin'."*

## From Slave to Capitalist, Philanthropist and Republican Party Leader

*He talked at length on the general situation and wound up with the following:*

*"I guess the country will get along all right anyhow, no matter who's elected. Of course I think Harrison will be, but if he aint an' Cleveland or Hill is, I guess I'll git erlong just de same. De day of bitterness is past, an' we all know de country is goin ter git erlong. Ef a democrat is elected you all will say you're glad, an' ef Harrison is elected you will say you were afraid so all de time, dat he wuz in office an' had a pull, an' was a pretty good president after all."*

Only four and a half months later, his wife's afflicted niece, Catherine, who Elbert and Harriet had raised, having no children of their own, inherited all of his estate. The only exceptions were for a year's income to his lawyer, Joseph H. Dismukes, and Dr. Bedford James Head, his former owner, who Elbert Head described in his will as "my old friend who in my darkest days was a true and faithful friend." The good doctor had returned to Americus from Forsyth to take care of him in his final days.

What happened to Elbert Head's vast estate? J.H. Dismukes, the lawyer, married Catherine Head on July 28, 1895, and inherited all the realty property upon her death May 23, 1897. Barely two months later, he married Osceola Cook and lived comfortably off the rental income until 1903. Then, people from Troy, Alabama, claiming to be Elbert Head's nieces and nephews, sued Dismukes for the estate. After fighting through the courts, J.H. Dismukes voluntarily declared bankruptcy and died shortly thereafter on August 21, 1905, ironically, sitting on his front porch across Lee from the former Elbert Head home. In January 1906, the estate of the late Elbert Head was sold at public auction.

At Eastview Cemetery, where a mile-long funeral procession with two thousand mourners accompanied all that was mortal of Elbert Head to his final resting place, the Dismukes family plot is graced with several monuments. Despite provisions in both of their wills, neither the graves of Elbert Head nor his niece, Catherine, were marked. In the last year or two, the Sumter Historic Trust, Inc. has placed a proper and fitting memorial at the cemetery that reads thusly:

ELBERT HEAD
SEPT. 7, 1817
OCT. 30, 1892
CAPITALIST PHILANTHROPIST
REPUBLICAN PARTY LEADER

# Georgia's First Female Doctor

I offer for your edification a biographical sketch of the first Sumter County woman honored by Wesleyan College and its Georgia Women of Achievement award. Her induction ceremony was on March 11, 1993, at Wesleyan's Porter Auditorium. Her co-inductees were Mary Musgrove, Oglethorpe's translator in the Georgia colony, Gertrude P. "Ma" Rainey, better known as the "Mother of the Blues," Viola R. Napier, first woman elected to the State House of Representatives, and Dicksie B. Bandy, who started the textile industry in Dalton and was responsible for the restoration of the Vann House, a tribute to the Cherokee Nation.

Galvanized by an April 1988 speech by First Lady Rosalynn Carter on the importance of recognizing the role of women in the history of Georgia, the Georgia Women of Achievement award's official mission statement is as follows: "Georgia Women of Achievement will recognize and honor women native to or clearly identified with the state of Georgia, who have made extraordinary contributions within their fields of endeavor and concern, and who will thus inspire future generations to utilize their own talents. Each recipient of the Georgia Women of Achievement award shall have been deceased at least ten years prior to her selection."

Cassandra Pickett Windsor Durham, of the Plains of Dura, was the first woman to earn a medical degree in the state of Georgia, perhaps the first in the entire South. She was born May 21, 1824, in Fairfield District, South Carolina, a daughter of John Jeptha Pickett Sr. and Nancy Boulware. She was known affectionately to her family as Kisannah, after her maternal grandmother. She reached adulthood in Stewart County, Georgia, and married, on November 6, 1845, Jonathan Windsor, a member of the family for whom the hotel is named.

Several sources, all apparently rooted in the same reference, claim she married a Pickett cousin first. However, no marriage license or estate record supports that claim. As she was twenty-one at the time of her marriage to Jonathan Windsor, the normal marrying age in those days, it is my considered opinion that Windsor was her first husband.

The two families intermarried again when her brother, Jeptha Boulware Pickett, married her sister-in-law, Mary Windsor, on December 14, 1848. Jonathan Windsor died in 1851 and Cassandra apparently remarried in Webster County about 1854. There is no license for this marriage in either Stewart or Sumter, and Webster, carved out of Stewart in 1853, lost its early records to a courthouse fire in 1914.

Cassandra's second husband, Dr. John Pryor Durham, set the stage for her historic claim to fame. For over a decade and a half, she accompanied him on his ministrations to the sick, all the while developing an affinity for the healing arts. His practice covered Dooly, Sumter and Webster, requiring travel to his patients on horseback or by horse and buggy. Cassandra seemed to have an innate gift for nursing; she, too, often rode horseback.

When Dr. J.P. Durham died at Bottsford, formerly a town on the Sumter-Webster line southwest of Plains, on December 9, 1869, (he reposes in an unmarked grave at that community's Old Rural Hill Methodist Church cemetery), Cassandra and her family were left with a trunk full of then worthless Confederate money and $200 in gold.

Bottsford and the Plains of Dura were bereft of a doctor and Cassandra Durham only had about a year's income. The membership of the Baptist, Methodist and Universalist churches in that section took care of her four children while she went to the Reform Medical College of Georgia, then located on Mulberry Street in Macon. The institution was originally chartered in 1839 as the Southern-Botanica-Medical College, at Forsyth, but removed to Macon in 1854. It relocated to Atlanta in 1881.

Returning to Sumter County and taking up residence in Americus, Dr. Cassandra Durham began the practice of botanic eclectic medicine, often gathering her own herbs in the swamps near Americus and compounding her own prescriptions. The *Weekly Sumter Republican* of March 17, 1871, literally heralded her arrival in Americus: "Mrs. C. Durham, Doctress in Medicine, is a professional acquisition to the city, whose services are offered to the sick and afflicted." The 1880 federal census of Americus also identified her occupation as "doctress."

How did the local community respond to a female doctor? It depends on whom you believe. According to Daisy O. Mallard in the *Tri-County News* of November 9, 1944, "it is told that other doctors objected vigorously to having a woman practicing medicine here and that a keen rivalry existed between them." This opinion was based on hearsay six decades removed. Charles W. Hancock, in the *Weekly Sumter Republican* of March 17, 1882, noted that "We have here in Americus a lady who is a graduate of a Medical College and we have seen her diploma…Mrs. Durham has been practicing in and near this city for several years and is quite successful, and has as good knowledge of medicine as most of the gentlemen who practice. She commands the respect of every gentleman and lady of this section and is doing a good business."

Dr. Durham lived in several different homes during her residence here. She even spent part of the decade in Preston, where she could "be found during the day at her office on the East side of the square, and at her residence near Mr. James Bell in the night." It was a different bell in the night that cost her the diploma she rightly cherished. On April 11, 1878, a massive fire broke out in the three-story city hall building on the northeast corner of Cotton Avenue and Lamar Street. Her rented residence, immediately east, was one of four wooden structures lost to the fire. Next east after the fourth wooden building, J.P. Chapman's three-year-old brick building, the Ruby Bar and Restaurant, prevented the fire's advance upon the rest of the city. This is the structure currently nearing completion after a yearlong rehabilitation.

On October 18, 1885, while attending her patient, Mrs. Sallie Paine, at Ward's Station (now Shellman), in Randolph County, she died suddenly from an attack of apoplexy and was buried there. In another of those delicious ironies one finds so often while studying history, like her husband, her final resting place is unmarked.

At least four successive generations of the family carried on the medical tradition. Here in Americus some of our oldest readers will remember her grandchildren, Mr. and Mrs. Howe Durham, first cousins, who owned and operated Durham Iron Company, along with a truck and equipment business, both here and in Albany.

Cassandra Pickett Windsor Durham's graduation speech has fortunately survived by transcription. It had been copied into a ledger book by a near relative, Micajah Boulware Pickett. I found her remarks to be socially progressive, sexually enlightened and, as to her own final disposition, even prophetic. See if you agree.

> *Ladies and Gentlemen: In conformity to the usages and customs of this college I address you. Not, however, upon the themes usually discussed, but upon a theme that is more difficult to treat successfully and satisfactorily than a mere thesis upon the nature and treatment of physical disease.*
>
> *It is with the mind of the public, the prejudices of the world, and with the newness of the effort by me to inaugurate a New Era in the practice of medicine in the South.*
>
> *In order to properly appreciate the difficulties that surround me, you have but to view me as a woman, alone and helpless, but*

*determined to inaugurate a New Era in the medical profession for the benefit of my sex.*

*From time immemorial we have, by the powers that be, and the prejudices of man, been denied the right to minister to the wants of our own sex as practicing physicians.*

*From the earlier ages of the world man has frowned upon the idea of lady physicians and has monopolized to himself the sole legal right to pry in to the nature and treatment of diseases peculiar to women, thus stultifying and blunting the finer feelings of her nature which distinguish her from the opposite sex and make her lovely and attractive to men.*

*Such has been the general history of WOMAN. But I am (I repeat) to say that in every age of the world there have been isolated cases where women, sustained by a few generous souled men, and the encouraging smiles of friends, have risen to the very top round of the ladder of fame in every department of life.*

*Thus have they proven to the world that God in his wisdom and goodness has created us self-reliant, self-sustaining, and useful members of our society—not mere drones in the community, nor baubles to be cared for by a man in his leisure hours.*

*When we take a retrospective view of the past, and scan narrowly the history of its despotisms, we find that in the long line of kings and queens who have reigned from the time of the Queen of Sheba to that of Victoria of England, there have been as many eminent queens as kings according to numbers. Queens who have proven themselves capable of governing successfully and prosperously.*

*This proves to us that God has not made women to live lives of ease, but that he has endowed them with power and capabilities which, when fully developed and properly directed, present them to the world women of full stature in knowledge and wisdom, and capable of discharging the many duties which devolve upon them as helpmeets for man.*

*In the literary and scientific world thousands of authoresses are known to have shown themselves capable of rivaling success-*

*fully the ablest of male authors, both in chasteness of style, and in force of diction or expression.*

*In our female novelists we find a thorough knowledge of human nature. And yet the female sex has, in the past, from false notions of propriety and refinement, been denied their rightful privilege of entering the medical profession where they might fully minister to the wants of their own sex, whose real physical condition may never be clearly and fully comprehended by the male physicians.*

*Not by reason of incapacity upon the part of the physician. But women find it hard to subdue those long nourished feelings of reticence which characterize her for modesty. She cannot unbosom herself fully as to her condition in those diseases peculiar to her sex.*

*The thousands of emaciated forms of humanity—mere wrecks of womanhood—that today are breathing out a lingering existence upon earth, is no evidence of incompetency upon the part of the male physicians.*

*It does prove, however, that that refined and long cultivated modesty that adorns a woman must be blunted, or a physician of her own sex must be supplied—a physician whose sympathy for her patient will insure that degree of confidence that will enable her to arrive at a true diagnosis of the disease to be treated. For upon a true diagnosis of the disease depends, of course, a successful treatment of the case.*

*By way of illustrating the force of the ideas expressed, I deem it sufficient to call your attention to the results achieved by the organization and labor of the Sisters of Charity. Without the right to practice as physicians, they have, as mere attendants upon the sick, and through the sympathy existing for other women, been enabled to learn facts which, when imparted to the attending physician, gave him power to diagnose and treat successfully the disease.*

*Ladies and gentlemen, such are the facts which prompt me willingly to encounter the trials and difficulties which I know must follow my feeble efforts to inaugurate a New Era in the medical profession.*

*Even a failure upon my part will not call forth one regret in regard to this undertaking. Success may not bring forth one approving smile to encourage me in my lone labors. Yet I have the greatest encouragement in a pure and exalted desire to confer a benefit upon my own sex.*

*My failure would not be the last effort made in this great reform. More brilliant intellects, with superior advantages, will rise up in the future and consummate the great and noble work commenced in 1870.*

*And this College and this Faculty will have the honor of first practically acknowledging the rights of women to enter this profession. And you, gentlemen, will have the proud satisfaction of knowing that your lectures and your counsels have not been in vain. That your disinterested friendship to a lone reformer was like bread cast upon the waters—bread that will be gathered up many days hence in the form of greater privilege for Southern women.*

*Years may pass and the beginner of this reform will be laid low in the dust. No marble column may mark her resting place, but in the towns and cities of the South, infirmaries and homes for the destitute sick will be found and recognized as standing monuments to the ultimate success of the reform now begun.*

*To the young gentlemen who have attended these lectures I wish to say that your conduct in the presence of a female auditor has been all that modesty and decorum demands. The appreciation of your conscience and the approving smile of Heaven will be your highest reward.*

*To the gentlemen composing this faculty I can only say that you have my most sincere thanks for the treatment I have received at your hands. My sojourn among you as a learner has been both pleasant and instructive.*

*Again, I thank you.*

# "A True Type of the Proud, Chivalric Gentleman"

Allen Sherrod Cutts was a major player in the development of Americus and Sumter County during the second half of the nineteenth century, despite the fact that he was not native to our area. He was born on December 4, 1826, in Pulaski County, Georgia. His father, Major Joseph Sherrod Cutts, was an English immigrant who had settled in North Carolina with, in turn, his parents, Henry Sherrod and Mary Ann Cutts. They were described as "slave-owning planters, and of large means." There is some dispute about the spelling of the middle name. A descendant informed me some years ago that it is spelled with one "r" but all the contemporaneous accounts from Cutts's own lifetime employ the spelling above.

Major Joseph S. Cutts moved to Georgia as a young man, setting up residency in Warren County. He served in the War of 1812 and married Elizabeth Maddux in 1824 in Hancock County. She was a daughter of Judge John Thomas Maddux and his wife, the former Sarah Betts. They were from Maryland but had become one of Georgia's most prominent families.

As a boy, Allen S. Cutts grew up in Pulaski, Randolph, Houston, Stewart and Sumter counties. During the family's stay in Randolph, Major J.S. Cutts died in 1843. According to A.S. Cutts's obituary years later, his "boyhood days were spent on the farm near Friendship, and though only a common school education was allowed him his natural attainments well equipped him for the long and useful life that followed."

At the age of only nineteen years Allen Cutts enlisted in the U.S. Army for service in the Mexican American War of 1846–48. He entered as a private but rose quickly through the ranks and served as lieutenant of artillery. By the close of hostilities he had attained the rank of captain and reached his own majority. This experience would stand him in good stead for what was to follow almost a decade and a half later.

In the interim, A.S. Cutts began his civilian career by clerking in mercantile establishments. He started his own business in Oglethorpe in 1851 when it was the terminus of the South Western (later Central) Railroad. Secure in the knowledge that the railroad was being extended to Americus, Allen Cutts and the railroad arrived in Sumter County in 1854. From a personal perspective it was an eventful year, as he also married Miss Fannie O. Brown, of Monroe County, on June 17, 1854. A daughter of James V. Brown, a prosperous planter of that county, she bore her husband seven children, four of whom survived his passing: Claude S., Ernest A., Eldridge H. and Miss Inez Cutts. In 1855 he bought two and a half acres for $200 on the south side of what was then Bridge Street and built the house still located at 416 West Church Street. Just two months earlier he had paid $4,900 for seven slaves, Boy, Joe, Sampson, Elbert, Sam, Nancy and one child. The following year he purchased a farm in the seventeenth district near Croxton's Crossroads and became a planter, dealing in cotton during the fall season.

He must have made quite an impression, as the voters of Sumter County elected him sheriff for the years 1856–57. After his one term in that office, A.S. Cutts moved to Florida where he engaged very successfully in railroad construction, building one of the then largest lines in that state, for which he received grants to nearly three hundred thousand acres of valuable land. While there he played no small part in an incident of some significance in American history.

The *Times-Recorder* of August 26, 1937, carried the following story as related by Professor James E. Mathis, the city's longtime school superintendent and former mayor:

> *While the importation of slaves had been forbidden long before the War between the States, yet there were adventurous souls who were willing to take the chance where the profit was large and, like liquor in the Volstead days, slaves were bootlegged past the guards along the coast.*
>
> *The last slaver was a vessel called the* Wanderer, *fitted by Charles Lamar of Savannah and W.G. Currie of New York, who brought a cargo of slaves from Africa and attempted to make Charleston, SC.*
>
> *A U.S. patrol ship gave chase when the* Wanderer *outran her, going down the coast, beached on Jekyll Island, opened the hatches and let these wild men out into the island jungle.*
>
> *When the government vessel came up a hawser was fastened to the* Wanderer *which was declared confiscated and carried away. As soon as the government officials had gone, track dogs were procured and the negroes caught.*
>
> *Allen S. Cutts had taken a contract to grade a part of the old F.C. & P.R.R. running from River Junction to Jacksonville, Fla. He bought the slaves and put them to work on this railroad grading.*
>
> *The negro's natural way of carrying a burden is on his head even until today, but these poor heathens knew no other way so they proceeded to get under the wheelbarrows, which were used almost exclusively in the old days of railroad construction in Florida.*
>
> *Colonel Cutts was the leading cotton man...of Americus at that time. At the outbreak of the War between the States, he organized an artillery company and went to Virginia as its captain. The company was soon recruited to the strength of a regiment*

*with Cutts still in command as colonel. Under this dashing com-*
*mander it soon gained the distinctive title of The Flying Artillery.*
*He was every inch a soldier and looked the part, the idol of every*
*man who served under him.*

Allen Cutts returned to Americus in 1858 just in time to join with Timothy M. Furlow and Willis A. Hawkins in financing the construction of the Furlow Masonic Female College on South Jackson Street, which opened the following year. His commitment to education would also be evidenced when he served as a charter member of the Americus board of education when it was formed in 1873.

As the decade of the 1850s came to a close, A.S. Cutts and his next-door neighbor and business partner, William L. Johnson, under the firm name of Cutts & Johnson, conducted a substantial cotton enterprise in Americus, but it would be short-lived. With the outbreak of the Civil War in April 1861 both men enlisted in the Confederate cause, each as a commander of his own outfit.

On July 6, 1861, Captain Allen S. Cutts organized the Sumter Flying Artillery and, after their arrival in Richmond, Virginia, nine days later, they were equipped with guns captured at the recent battle of first Manassas. According to *Who Was Who in the Confederacy*, Volume II, by Stewart Sifakis, Cutts's assignments included major, artillery (May 22, 1862); commanding an artillery battalion, reserve artillery, army of Northern Virginia (May 22, 1862–June 2, 1863); lieutenant colonel, artillery (May 26, 1862); and commanding artillery battalion, Third Corps, army of Northern Virginia (June 2, 1863–early 1865).

The Sumter Flying Artillery's battle flag has its own unique history. It was designed by Mrs. Mary T. Elam, the premier milliner of Americus. During the final days of the war, as the army of Northern Virginia retreated from Richmond, the Sumter Artillery covered the rear guard. On April 8, 1865, General George A. Custer (yes, *that* General Custer) and his cavalry overran Battery A and bugler Charles Schorn, of Company M, First West Virginia Calvary, captured the flag. For this, he was awarded the Medal of

Honor after the war. The U.S. War Department (now Department of Defense) returned the banner to the state of Georgia in 1905, along with twenty-five others. My friend and fellow student of local history, state Senator George B. Hooks, played a significant role in the final disposition of the battered relic. As the then chairman of the Senate Appropriations Committee, he provided the funding for the flag's renovation and placement of honor in the state capitol.

At the battle of Dranesville on December 20, 1861, Captain A.S. Cutts was noticed by his commander, General J.E.B. Stuart, actually loading the cannons himself, and was singled out and described by Stuart as the "brave, true, heroic" Cutts. The Eleventh Georgia Artillery Battalion, which came to be known variously as the Sumter Battalion or Cutts's Battalion, was organized in late May 1862 with the addition of three new companies formed in Sumter and surrounding counties. The original Sumter Battery became Company A of the newly constituted battalion.

After his promotion to command of the Sumter Battalion, Lieutenant Colonel A.S. Cutts led his men in the Peninsula Campaign and at the battles of Sharpsburg on September 17, 1862, (where they provided artillery support for Confederate forces defending the Bloody Lane in the center of the line) and Chancellorsville (on May 1–4, 1863). He also saw action in the battles of Fredericksburg on December 13, 1862, and Gettysburg on July 1–3, 1863. In the latter three-day battle, which most historians consider the turning point of the war, Cutts's Artillery was situated atop Seminary Ridge in a constant exchange with Union guns at Cemetery Hill. They also provided cover for the retreat across the Potomac River. During 1864, from the Wilderness, on May 5–6, to Petersburg, Lieutenant Colonel Cutts distinguished himself and his unit by fending off the Union attack of June 20 at the latter place. Actually, he commanded two battalions simultaneously throughout that final campaign.

Despite spending four years in the very heart of some of the most sanguinary battles of that vicious conflict, Allen Cutts received only a slight wound and was sick at home in Americus when the surrender came at Appomattox Courthouse, Virginia.

For the remainder of his life, Colonel A.S. Cutts devoted himself to the cotton business and public service. In October 1865 he was a member of the constitutional convention at the then state capital of Milledgeville. Over the next three decades he would serve as mayor of Americus for the years 1874–75, 1877–78 and 1893–96. He and John B. Felder, another Confederate veteran, basically alternated occupying the mayoralty during that span of years. At the earnest behest of the Alliancemen of Sumter County, a political association representing farmers' interests, Colonel Cutts was elected as our state representative for the 1890–91 term.

During his final term as mayor, Colonel Allen S. Cutts's useful and productive life came to an end. Late on the night of March 17, 1896, at his home on Brown Street, he died peacefully and calmly. The house, incidentally, remains but was moved to Horne Street in 1912 when the John W. Sheffield family built the large burnt-brick structure on its former site.

The funeral was conducted by Reverend T.M. Christian at the Methodist Church with military, civic and Masonic honors. The pallbearers consisted of Dr. Erwin J. Eldridge and William A. Dodson, Esquire, from the board of education; John E. Sullivan and Malcolm B. Council, from DeMolay Commandery No. 5, Knights Templar; Christopher J. Sherlock and James F. Bolton, from the city council; and William M. McGarrah and Thomas A. Graham, from Cutts's Battalion.

As his obituary noted, "Col. Allen S. Cutts was a Georgian by birth and a true type of the proud, chivalric gentleman of the old South…Americus can ill afford the loss of such a man as Col. Cutts. He was loved, honored and trusted by everyone, for few possessed such traits of character. Possessed of a strong mind he formed firm opinions, which he never feared to express, though these were always tempered with justice and charity. Brave, honest and true, he was in every respect a model man and citizen and his place will indeed be hard to fill."

# "An Unwarranted Act of Brutality and Barbarism"

On the summer solstice in the year 1913 the sun shone on Americus and a scene of such horror and depravity as to make any decent human being want to deny its very existence. The duty we have as students of history is that we record, and learn from, all past events, whether good or bad. Sometimes history is just plain ugly and we have to face that simple fact.

I refer you, gentle reader, to the famous George Santayana quote, "Those who cannot remember the past are condemned to repeat it." The wisest among us learn from our mistakes; but if we are ignorant of those mistakes and their historical context how, then, can we learn in order to avoid repeating them?

As to the relevance of this subject, my more discerning readers have probably already figured out what must have happened here. However, let me supply a little historical context first. The late 1800s and early 1900s were pretty much awful in the South as far as racial relations were concerned. It was a time of "separate but equal" and "white supremacy" as the guiding dogmas of that era. The former was rigidly separate but inherently unequal while the latter was based on no scientific or religious foundation.

During this period in Georgia's history, Atlanta experienced a two-day race riot in 1906, the Leo Frank case arose in 1913, and

Buchanan Corner at Cotton and Lamar in 1913.

the Ku Klux Klan had their massive revival on Stone Mountain in 1915. In the middle of all that, on June 21, 1913, Americus was the scene of one of the state's most brutal lynchings. Our beloved Georgia, by the way, was surpassed only by Mississippi and Texas in total numbers of this particularly vicious crime against humanity. Citizens of each of these states perpetrated over four hundred of these wanton acts of violence in the century from the 1860s to the 1960s.

Here is what happened in our fair city, at that time still the eighth largest in the state. At 6:30 on a Saturday evening on the longest day of the year, business was still being transacted uptown, specifically at W.D. Bailey's clothier shop on the northeast corner and Buchanan's Grocery on the northwest corner of the intersection of Cotton and Lamar.

A small group of black men were congregating outside both establishments when police Chief William Cyrus Barrow came by and advised them to move along. One of them, Will Redding, apparently balked at that and Chief Barrow arrested him for noncompliance. As he was being led away, Redding, about twenty-four-years-old and of large physique, got into a struggle with Barrow, a sixty-eight-year-old Confederate veteran, and two other citizens who tried to subdue him.

Despite being clubbed by Barrow's pistol, Redding grabbed the old soldier's gun, broke away, and then ran across Cotton towards Buchanan's corner. As Barrow advanced upon him, Redding turned and, holding the weapon with both hands, shot the chief through the ribcage, piercing the liver. The bullet exited from the back and struck Morris Allen, the black porter for the Ayashery, who was standing directly behind Chief Barrow. Allen suffered a minor flesh wound on his left arm.

Will Redding, realizing where he was and what he had just done, took off running north on Cotton Avenue with a crowd of irate citizens, led by Arthur Rylander, chasing and firing at him. At Wheeler Street, across from Turpin's Stable, Redding turned and fired at his pursuers but struck Daniel Stallings, an innocent black bystander who had stepped into the line of fire. Stallings would be the third individual to lose his life as a result of what transpired that day.

Behind the Southern Express Co., one block from Cotton on Wheeler, Will Redding was shot and overpowered. After the arrival of Sheriff Quitman Washington Fuller and Deputy Lucius Harvey in their car, he was immediately rushed to the county jail then situated on the elevation behind the present location of Citizens Bank of Americus. There, the prisoner was placed in a cell on the second floor of the castle-like structure.

As the courthouse clock next door tolled 8:00 p.m., a mob of several hundred men and boys filled in the open space between the jail and Lee Street. At this juncture, Reverend James B. Lawrence, rector of Calvary Episcopal Church, and Reverend John W. Stokes, of First Presbyterian Church, appealed to the mob's leaders not to carry out their murderous plan. Brother Lawrence was picked up

*Left to right*: Sumter County courthouse and jail, Americus city hall and water tower in the 1890s.

bodily by members of the crowd and passed over their heads until he was set down on Lee Street. Armed with crowbars and massive hammers, the mob took about twenty minutes to break down the steel doors since Sheriff Fuller had refused to give them his keys.

Will Redding was snatched from his cell and dragged out onto Forsyth Street where he was beaten to death, or nearly so, with a crowbar. The mob, now in full blood lust, dragged his body up Forsyth towards Cotton. A local newspaper described them thusly, "wild-eyed, sweating, panting sons of chaos, pushing, pulling and punching shoulder to shoulder with other howling, cursing maniacs."

Ladies exiting Dudley's Theater, above the now Rib Rack, were confronted with the harrowing sight unfolding below them. My great-aunt, Miss Nannie E. Speer, was on that stairwell searching the crowd for her brother, Callie. My uncle, Gilly Purvis, who passed away July 20, 2003, remembered the event as he, his Uncle Callie and the rest of the family were afraid to leave their home at 606 East Church Street. Gilly and his cousin, Judson Rushin, hid under their beds.

Upon the arrival at the scene of the crime back at Buchanan's corner, four members of the lynch mob climbed the telephone pole and tried unsuccessfully to lift the body "to a point sufficiently high to permit of shooting him without endangering the lives of any others." Redding's considerable weight made this too difficult so they tried hanging him from a cable reaching across Cotton, but the rope broke.

During the ensuing delay, as the leaders of the mob discussed among themselves how to best complete their horrific act, Reverend Robert L. Bivins of what was then Furlow Lawn Baptist Church (now Central Baptist) approached them. As with Brother Lawrence, he, too, was rebuffed in his attempts to halt their efforts.

A stronger rope had been secured and Redding's now lifeless body was hoisted to the top of the telephone pole, where it was exposed for twenty minutes to a withering fire of over a thousand rounds by men and boys on the scene after someone had given the command to "Aim high and shoot!" Members of the mob loaded and reloaded their pistols, firing so many bullets that Redding's corpse was completely denuded. As was noted in the newspaper, "hundreds of spectators watched from the sidewalks the gruesome and horrible spectacle."

The final indignity occurred with the cutting down of the body. As it lay in the street some depraved individuals removed body parts for souvenirs. My cousin, Bobby Peacock, was visited at his antique shop by a customer from Florida some years ago. The gentleman was inquiring about this incident since he owned one of those souvenirs! The corpse was subsequently drenched in kerosene oil and set afire. The odious smell of burning flesh caused many spectators to leave the scene and the fire department arrived on the scene to extinguish the flames. Believe it or not, they were concerned the burning corpse might ignite the wooden block street.

Governor Joseph M. Brown ordered the Americus Light Infantry, under the command of Captain James A. Fort, to patrol the streets of the city but by the time they assembled at 11:00 p.m. all was calm and serene. Nevertheless, they maintained their posted positions throughout the night.

On Sunday morning every church in the city condemned the mob violence of the previous evening. Congregations at First Methodist, First Presbyterian and Calvary Episcopal unanimously arose in opposition to mob rule. First Baptist and Furlow Lawn Baptist adopted written resolutions, the former expressing "abhorrence and disapproval" and the latter characterizing it all as an "unwarranted act of brutality and barbarism by some who dwell among us."

The city's two newspapers joined in the condemnation. Frank T. Long, editor of the *Times-Recorder*, denounced "the lynching as an offense against humanity, against civilization, and a grievous offense against the law-loving and law-abiding people of Americus...that here, as in all communities where lynchings have occurred, the crime of lynching was perpetrated by the thoughtless, the unrestrained, and criminally inclined element found in this community, as in others." Editor Clarence A. Ames of the *South Georgia Progress* announced "our contempt for the men who openly encouraged, by intemperate speech and otherwise, the defiance of peace and good order and the process of law, who were yet too cowardly and ashamed to take an active part. As to the mob itself, we pause, bewildered, astonished...isn't it a spectacle tended to dwarf one's conception of Christianity and education and morality?"

Superior Court Judge Zera A. Littlejohn convened a grand jury investigation on June 30. During the interim, despite a valiant attempt on his part, Chief W.C. Barrow passed away at his home, on Jackson Street opposite the Presbyterian Church, six days after the shooting.

The grand jury consisted of J.W. Timmerman, foreman, and R.P. Stackhouse, E.D. Sheffield, S.A. Daniels, J.W. Clopton, F.G. Janes, J.G. Feagin, B.L. Dell, A.J. Conyers, F.P. Harrold, E.C. Webb, J.T. Methvin, J.H. Miers, J.E. Poole, T.M. Lowery, W.E. Brown, S.E. Statham, Ross Dean, C.S. Hogg, J.T. McLendon, J.S. Johnson, E.L. Bell and A.B. Conners. Despite four days of testimony from 150 witnesses, including the sheriff and members of the police department, no one could positively identify any of the participants in the grisly affair.

## "An Unwarranted Act of Brutality and Barbarism"

Ironically, J.W. Furlow, the *Times-Recorder*'s chief correspondent, had written the following: "There was no attempt whatever at concealment upon the part of those participating, as not a man wore a mask of any kind."

# Sumter County's Antebellum Courthouse

Our pioneer ancestors might have been alerted to what would turn out to be a rocky first half century with the county's initial attempt at raising a courthouse. In 1834 the Inferior Court, precursors to our county commission, hired John R. Moore as contractor for the construction of a large, two-story wood frame structure to be situated in the middle of the square bounded by Forsyth, Jackson, Lamar and Troup (now Lee) Streets, the city's first four. He appropriated $950, half of the cost, and promptly left town having built nothing. During its actual construction over the next five years the courthouse was used ecumenically by the Baptists and Methodists before they could establish their own sanctuaries. After being rolled to the west side of the square in 1851 and serving as a hotel for thirteen years, it was lost to the great fire of August 30, 1864.

A national economic depression, which hit farmers the hardest, resulted in several farmers' revolts in various counties in Georgia. We are fortunate to have an eyewitness account of the proceedings right here in Americus on May 2 and 3, 1842. The first is a letter from a lawyer attending the public sale and the second is the grand jury's response to the behavior of some of our local citizens.

From the *Macon Telegraph* of May 10, 1842:

*The hour for the Sheriff's sale arrived, and the Court suspended business to give him an opportunity to sell. Mr. McCrary, the Deputy Sheriff, proceeded to the door of the Court House and proclaimed that the sale would then commence and began to read from the advertisement, when three or four strong men seized him and carried him off, viet armis! Judge Taylor upon being informed of this affair, repaired immediately to the Court House and ordered the Sheriff (Ebenezer J. Cottle) to summon a sufficient guard, and to arrest the mob who had carried off the Deputy by violence—which was accordingly done, and some two or three were overtaken and arrested, and stand indicted by special presentment for resisting the officer, etc. The Sheriff then proceeded to sell (or rather to attempt to sell). The people were harangued by some man, whom I could not see, forewarning persons present not to bid for property. It is impossible to tell how many were determined to prevent a sale—unless to suppose that a majority acquiesced in it. One man I saw, who with a most barbarous look and gesture, absolutely forbade any bidding whatever. I knew him not, but I never shall forget his visage. A mad wild cat could not have looked more demon like—his teeth gritted as he spoke, and he shook his head and threatened that the man who dared to bid should be well mobbed! The man was a stranger to me. I was interested in the Sheriff's sale, but felt that if I bid, it would be at the peril of my life. Some eight or ten stood round as spokesmen, and as the Sheriff would offer an article of property for sale, they would say "no bid." So that out of an advertisement of two or three columns in a newspaper, the Sheriff sold but two tracts of land—one for five dollars and the other for fifty, which was permitted, as it was only to perfect titles. Judge Taylor met this crisis with firmness and decision, and called upon the Grand Jury, as the right arm of the criminal law, to present all those who were engaged deterring others from bidding. Excuse haste, and believe me to be your friend, etc.*

*JAMES M. KELLY*

Presentment of the Grand Jury of Sumter County May Term 1842:

> *That our Temple of Justice has been <u>defamed</u>, that the laws of our county have been <u>desecrated</u>, that the civil authorities of the county have been threatened & violently seized upon (but not awed) are facts abhorrent to the better feelings of any member of this body and for which no part of the community feels as deeply the injury & degradation cast upon the entire county by a few <u>lawless Marauders</u>, who are <u>without honor, character</u> or <u>moral feelings</u>. We therefore recommend & require that any good citizens of the county, lend their aid to the detection of the perpetrators, that they may be brought to suffer the penalty & be held up to the scorn & indignation they so richly merit.*
>
> *We also present the Clerk of our Sup[erior] Court for negligently leaving his desk containing the court papers for the present Term all night in the open Court house, the loss of which will cause much delay in the ends of Justice.*
>
> *In bringing our labours to a close & taking leave of his Honor Judge Taylor, we beg permission to tender him every assurance of our high regard for the able, impartial & "<u>Spirited</u>" manner in which he has presided during the present <u>Boisterous Term</u>. We also to the Solicitor General A.A. Robinson tender our thanks for his kind attention to this body.*

That negligent superior court clerk was my great-great-great-grandfather Jacob W. Cobb and, coincidentally, the affair occurred on my birthday.

Not only were our pioneers passionate about their purse strings, they also pursued politics proactively. The presidential election of 1844 consisted of two political parties, the Democrats and the Whigs. Montgomery M. Folsom, after interviewing participants, wrote the following in the *Weekly Recorder* of September 11, 1885:

Antebellum Sumter County Courthouse (1853–1888).

*At an early hour on that memorable day men came pouring in from every direction. The little log hotels were crowded, and the liquor shops were alternately invaded by little knots of either political faction. As the day advanced the angry discussions became more frequent. At length they began to mass themselves in the courthouse yard. Each faction began to gather around its leader like a swarm of bees around the queen. Then a fisticuff began between two champions, and in a twinkling the great crowd was a mass of yelling, cursing, biting and gouging humanity. Every other man was armed with a stout hickory cudgel, and these were used with such effect that the majority of the combatants left the gory field with cuts and bruises about their heads and bodies, with now and then a veteran minus an ear, an eye or a section of nose. Men of Pondtown, men of Danville, men of Starkville and men of Americus found themselves with battered noses, bleeding heads and blackened eyes, hatless, shirtless, tattered and torn. It was a day to be remembered by both combatants and spectators.*

In May of 1853 Patrick Adams, the contractor, completed our second courthouse, the first made of brick. It is this edifice you see in the accompanying picture, a tintype taken about 1873. The original was donated to the clerk's office in 1949 by Mrs. W.H. Estes. Of the two men in the picture, Joseph H. Allen and John B. Pilsbury, the former was her ancestor and he served as superior court clerk from 1873 to 1901. Note, also, the little boy at the corner of the building whose ghost-like appearance resulted from his failure to stand still while the picture was being taken. The 1858 city clock was installed in the cupola of the courthouse in January 1867, much to the delight of editor C.W. Hancock.

Here the Georgia Supreme Court, Justices Lumpkin, Benning and Starnes, would hold their final session in Americus in July 1854. Some of the most prominent legal lights of the state attended that session, including Howell Cobb and his brother Thomas R.R. Cobb, Robert Toombs, Alexander H. Stephens and Charles Dougherty. Two local attorneys who tried cases in this courthouse, Henry K. McCay and Willis A. Hawkins, themselves later became associate justices of the Supreme Court. Two other lawyers residing here, General Philip Cook and Charles F. Crisp, went on to represent us in the U.S. Congress, the latter attain-

Victorian Sumter County Courthouse (1888–1959).

ing the status of Speaker of the House and the former afterward serving as Georgia's secretary of state. Of these members of the bar five have counties named in their honor.

In the social and political upheaval following the close of the Civil War, the courthouse was the scene of two other incidents that give us insight into the culture of those days. In October 1865, with a U.S. Army contingent bivouacked on the grounds of our present courthouse, former state representative and Americus mayor Thomas C. Sullivan, a retired attorney, shot with buckshot one of the soldiers for repeatedly depredating Sullivan's scuppernong vineyard on South Dudley Street. Although defended by A.R. Brown, H.K. McCay and W.J. Patterson at the military court martial, Sullivan was convicted and sentenced to a fine of $500 or five years in prison. Within a week local citizens, led by Colonel Allen S. Cutts, raised the fine and saved Sullivan.

Newly enfranchised black voters cast their first ballots at the courthouse in April 1868. Despite the rigidly segregated voting lines, U.S. troops had to relieve Captain John M. Shiver of his pistol when he showed up to cast his own ballot. I am fortunate to have his grandson, Willis, as my companion for lunch every Saturday at Granny's Kitchen.

When the antebellum brick courthouse was replaced by the Victorian beauty many older citizens will remember, the following bittersweet story appeared in the *Daily Times-Recorder* of October 11, 1891:

> *All that composed the old court house of Sumter county that has stood for many years in the center of the public square, has at last been torn away, and nothing now remains but the rubbish thereof.*
>
> *Shortly after the sketch written by Judge Pilsbury was published in the* Times-Recorder, *an old gentleman arrived in the city, and at once proceeded to the site where the building had stood.*
>
> *For several moments he stood silent and meditative, at length he spoke to a citizen, who was standing nearby, as follows:*

*"Thirty-five years ago, I was a citizen of this county, and a well-to-do farmer, living in the now Fifteenth district. I loved and married one of my neighbor's daughters, and for a short time life was worth living; I was supremely happy, and thanked our heavenly Father for the many blessings that he bestowed upon me and mine."*

*Here the old man pulled his handkerchief from his pocket and wiped away the tears that came trickling down his cheeks.*

*"Soon my happiness came to an end, and an unprincipled scoundrel came between my love and me. Weeks passed after this came to my knowledge before I spoke to my wife of my intentions, which were to sue for a divorce and leave the county. Court was in session. I came to Americus and employed Ad. Brown, who duly filed my complaint. But the court could not see things as I did, and would not grant me a divorce. I left the court house, vowing that I would never marry until the court house was either burned down or torn away. That vow I have kept; though it was hard to do. I left my wife, plantation and all, wandered over the west; fought through the war and courted death. After the war was over I settled in Terrell county and have lived there ever since."*

*At this time the old man's face brightened up and a smile took the place of tears as the citizen asks him what he was going to do. Said he: "I have kept my vow, and as the old house has been torn away, I will be married next Sunday afternoon. I came here to see if it was really gone. Yes sir, I will marry next Sunday afternoon."*

Such was life in a society where the courthouse was the center of attention.

# "A Woman of Substance"

Since retirement, I have been having breakfast at Burger King just about every morning. There is a regular cast of locals who do the same. On Thursdays, there is even a group of ladies who meet and chat weekly. Manager Beverly Dingle has spent twenty years creating what Ernest Hemingway deemed "a clean, well-lighted place."

One of the daily regulars is Jane Myers, along with her husband, Lamar, and she and I usually briefly discuss local history, since I am lucky enough to have her as a fan of my essays in the *Times-Recorder*. After my last effort, it occurred to me that her mother, the late Janet S. Merritt, would be a great subject for Women's History Month. Jane gracefully allowed me access to her mother's voluminous papers and that research is the basis of this essay.

Janet Burton Scarborough Merritt's family bloodline consisted of numerous lines back to the American Revolution, not only in Georgia but in South Carolina and Virginia as well. As a direct result, she would become prominent in the state and national Daughters of the American Revolution (DAR). Her various family connections read like a Who's Who of American history. Her father's Burtons were from Effingham County and her mother's Burtons were from Elbert and Wilkes counties. Both sets of Burtons had earlier migrated from Virginia.

Robert Burton Jr. was born in 1820 and moved, in the 1830s, to the portion of Lee County that would become Schley County in 1857. In 1842, he married Martha Ashurst Wilkinson, of Talbotton, Georgia, who was a sister-in-law of U.S. Senator Benjamin Harvey Hill. Of their two daughters, the eldest by one year, Ella Leila, was Janet Merritt's paternal grandmother. Ella's sister, Clara Belle, would become the wife of Charles Frederick Crisp, who later served as Speaker of the U.S. House of Representatives from 1891 to 1895 and was U.S. senator-elect when he died suddenly in 1896. Politics is a thread woven throughout the tapestry that is this family's history.

Both of the Burton sisters attended Wesleyan College during the Civil War, after a private education by a governess in their home, and it was there that Ella fell in love with Edward D. Amos, to whom she was married in September 1869. Within a year or so they were blessed with a little girl, Annie Claire, but then stricken by the death of the new husband and father. At age twenty-three, Ella B. Amos and her daughter, known to the younger generations as "Big Auntie" and "Little Auntie," moved back to her parents' home in Ellaville.

The town, incidentally, had been named for her in 1858 "because she was the prettiest girl in the county." The fact that her father had sold the 150 acres to the new county for the site of the courthouse square and other public buildings may have been of some consequence in that decision. The original community, located at the present Ellaville Cemetery, had been established as Pond Town circa 1812, with a federal post office designated in 1833.

On November 27, 1877, Ella married John Newton Scarborough, also of Schley County. He was the son of Reverend Dr. Henry Scarborough and the former Hulda Hudson. By the way, her brother, Leander Hudson, is interred under the obelisk at Founders Memorial Park in Americus. J.N. Scarborough's mother's family was active in politics as well. When Schley and Sumter were in the same state senate district, John Newton Hudson held the office for two years, 1878 and 1879. Thomas G. Hudson occupied the same office in 1902–04, then served as Georgia's commissioner of agriculture from 1905 to 1912.

"Judge" J.N. Scarborough was a lawyer, newspaper publisher, real estate agent and compiler of Americus's third city directory, issued on November 1, 1891. Two earlier ones had been published in 1869 and 1878. At the time of its publication the Scarborough family, with son Robert H. and daughters Stella and Leila, was residing west of the Speaker Crisp home on Taylor Street (*not* the one with the misplaced historic marker). The former Burton sisters were next-door neighbors. One year later, Arthur Rylander moved the one-story Scarborough residence to 222 Taylor so he could build his own two-story Victorian at its former address, now 214 Taylor, facing Barlow Street.

From 1892 to1897, during the second Democratic presidency of Grover Cleveland, John N. Scarborough served as postmaster for Americus. His was the first administration to occupy the newly constructed three-story edifice on Forsyth Street, which became the Bank of Commerce in 1910 and is now the Wachovia Bank building, although radically remodeled in 1961.

John and Ella Scarborough moved their family to what is now 112 East Church Street, across from the First United Methodist Church, the year before the Crisps were moving into their newly constructed home on Taylor Street in 1893 (the one *with* the misplaced historic marker). At their home on Church, according to family tradition, "Big Auntie" Ella Scarborough was the first woman to drive a car in Americus. It was a Baby Maxwell, with brass carriage-type lights on each side of the windshield, and had to be hand-cranked to get started.

John and Ella's son, Robert Henry Scarborough, married Janet Augusta Burton, of Athens, in that city on November 11, 1907. Their daughter, and eldest child, Janet Burton Scarborough, was born at her grandfather's house on January 4, 1909. Two years later they moved to Hawkinsville, but shortly thereafter received bad news.

On October 4, 1911, John Newton Scarborough succumbed to a lingering illness at his residence of the previous two decades. As she noted in her memoirs, Janet S. Merritt's earliest recollections were of her Grandpa Scarborough and that house. "Grandpa would come into the parlor once a day, never more often, and ceremoniously give me a stick of candy. I only got the one. I did not ask for another—I always wanted another, but for some strange reason I could not ask. It was a ceremony between the old man and me, and even then I must have sensed that culture is based upon the ritual, and that some things 'are done' and some 'are not done.'"

The old home place passed from the family's ownership after the death of Annie Claire "Little Auntie" Carter on November 21, 1931, "who was the last of the tribe to live there." She had earlier resided with her husband, Will C. Carter, at their two-story domicile on Lee Street that he had built in 1892, next to his father, Calvin W. Carter. A disastrous fire on November 9, 1917, destroyed not only the W.C. Carter place, but also the E.B. Council and W.G. Turpin homes immediately north of it. Ironically, Mrs. W.G. Turpin was the former Stella Scarborough, the niece of "Little Auntie." Barlow Council rebuilt the following year with a two-story brick residence that in recent years has been the office of Dr. Schley Gatewood Jr. The Pruitt Apartments replaced W.C. Carter's former home site in 1927.

J.N. Scarborough willed his law library to Janet's father and his mahogany and rosewood secretary to his granddaughter. Fortunately, the secretary stayed at the old home while the law books were lost to a fire that destroyed their Hawkinsville residence not long after the funeral and only two days after the birth of Janet's brother, John Augustus. As she was snatched from the burning structure, Janet grabbed her doll named Mary Jane and both the doll and the secretary remained for six decades in the brick-veneered home at 234 Dodson Street built by the Merritts in 1940.

Janet Scarborough's maternal grandmother, affectionately known as "Ma-ma," who was visiting them at the time of the conflagration, took her granddaughter to Athens on the train the very next day. She was the former Eliza Murrell Cobb, a scion of one of Georgia's most prominent families. All the Cobb family girls were given free tuition to the Lucy Cobb Institute and two of Janet's first cousins graduated from there, one of whom became one of the first women to make Phi Beta Kappa at the University of Georgia.

All through grammar and high school in Hawkinsville Janet took every opportunity to visit her Athens relatives who were "intimate with the old school of aristocrats and professors who made up the town in the twenties." She was convinced that this association was the most important thing in her early development, which subsequently fostered her interest in all things cultural.

Janet Scarborough's high school years in Hawkinsville ended with her graduation in 1926 as an honor student. The girls' final examination for their sewing class was to make their own graduation gowns and Janet won the cash prize for best made and designed one. It wasn't difficult as she had been sewing since she was five years old! Miss Lee Bennett, her mathematics and Latin teacher, admonished the girls against "shooting our mouths off too hastily" with the following quote, "Boys flying kites haul in their white winged birds, but you can't do that with spoken words," a lesson Janet never forgot. Her English classes were taught by Miss Ethel Adams, who later became Dean of Women at Milledgeville. Janet studied history under Miss Mae Michael, who was the sister of Miss Moina Belle Michael, "The Poppy Lady" who started the tradition that honors war veterans to this very day.

The new graduate had come to a crossroad. She would pursue a career in teaching but the question was which institute of teacher training to attend. Despite extensive family connections in Athens, Lucy Cobb was considering closing and the university and normal schools were not to her taste. Ultimately, she made her choice based on economic factors "with two others right on my heels and the Depression vaguely creeping up on us." She did three years worth of courses in a span of only two years at Georgia State Womans College in Valdosta, graduating on June 6, 1928.

Janet Scarborough's first teaching assignment was in a small town near Savannah with "boys too old to be in the seventh grade

**PREPARATION + OPPORTUNITY = SERVICE**
**And Add The Dividend Of EXPERIENCE!**

# JANET MERRITT

### Does All She Can,
### All The Time She Can
### For All
### The People She Can

★

### She Truly Represents
### "THE PEOPLE, YES!"

**HER CREDENTIALS ARE IN ORDER**

[This letter is used with permission of the writer. It was not written for campaign purposes.]

"Dear Mrs. Merritt,
Speaking as one of the newer citizens of our community, may I express our gratitude to you for the wonderful job you are doing for us, the citizens of Americus and Sumter County.
At times, the newcomers are the ones who see more clearly the progress being made in a community, and at the same time, see who is responsible for making this progress."

**Let's Re-Elect Representative JANET MERRITT,**
**Post 2, 46 District, September 9 Democratic Primary**

Political advertisement for state Representative Janet S. Merritt.

and silly giggling girls who made eyes at them." The next year she returned to Americus and taught for two years in the Sumter County school system but the salary left a great deal to be desired. As a consequence, she moved on to Terrell County for the following two years. During this transitional period, she met the man who would change her life.

Samuel Mickleberry Merritt was the son of Dr. Thomas M. Merritt Jr. and the former Berta McGarrah, descendants of pioneer families in the Friendship community as well as Americus. Their home in the city is still located at the southeast corner of College Street and Jackson Avenue and it was there that Samuel M. Merritt first saw the light of day on February 6, 1905. Both Merritts, father and son, were graduates of the University of Georgia. Sam was so smitten by the strong-willed young teacher that he spent three years hauling her around Sumter and Terrell counties. They were married on June 6, 1933, and eleven months and two weeks later celebrated the birth of their first child, Thomas Burton Merritt. He would be followed by the two girls, Mary Ella and Janet, the latter perhaps better known as Jane.

Hi Undercofler, who would later sit on the Georgia Supreme Court, including one year as its chief justice, announced his decision in April 1962 not to run for re-election to the General Assembly. Upon reading this in the *Times-Recorder*, Janet S. Merritt idly suggested to her husband that she would be interested in running for the seat. Much to her surprise, his response was "Go ahead. I'll pay your entrance fee. I think you would do a better job than any man I know." After nearly fainting, she accepted his offer and the next day went to the local Democratic chairman and paid the qualifying fee.

While many of Sumter's politicos, all men, were aghast at the thought of a woman running for state office, former Congressman Steve Pace disagreed. He arranged a meeting with the local labor committees from the railroad, the telephone company, Manhattan Shirt Factory and others to develop strategies and methods for the upcoming election. Janet Merritt narrowly lost to John W. Sewell, of Plains, an Alabama transplant who boasted of his connections to its governor, George C. Wallace.

In 1964 Janet Merritt returned the favor and defeated J.W. Sewell, with a little help from Governor Carl Sanders's political organization, as they were not thrilled with Sewell's constant campaign to get George Wallace to address the General Assembly. Another major factor in this victory was the voter turnout in the black community, which had just become enfranchised by the federal Civil Rights Act. She was the first local politician to actively campaign for their votes, instead of trying to buy their votes surreptitiously. Her daughter, Jane, organized her friends at Americus High School into a group called Merritt's Merry Maids and they campaigned door to door in Americus handing out cards and advertising matches.

When she went to Atlanta for the 1965 session of the General Assembly, Janet Merritt was the only woman in the state legislature. After re-apportionment, she was joined by Grace Hamilton of Atlanta, who was black. Male legislators joked that "If we've got to have women I suppose Janet Merritt is as good a white woman as we could have, and Grace Hamilton is as good a black woman as we could have." They were a caucus with only two members.

During her tenure in the state legislature from 1965 through 1972, Sumter County had two representatives. Janet Merritt served with Billy Blair in 1965–66, Clarence Parker 1967–1970 and Oliver Oxford 1971–72. Concurrently in her first two years, the county was represented in the state senate by an up and coming young politician, James Earl Carter Jr. He would enjoy no small success in the not too distant future.

Although Janet Merritt authored or co-authored over one hundred bills, she will always be remembered by the open-minded as a profile in courage for her 1969 attempt to change the state flag. As Georgia's state regent for the DAR at their national convention, she had noticed other states' delegates reacting negatively to the Confederate battle flag occupying two-thirds of our state flag. She was a dedicated student of history and, as such, was commit-

Merritt's Merry Maids in October 1964. *Left to right*: Grace Durham, Jane Merritt, Claudia McDuffie, Nancy Powell, Jeanette Sheppard, Linda Lansford, Betty Ann Buchanan, Betsy Bryant, Darlene Holliday.

ted to removing the racially inflammatory symbol and reinstating the 1879 flag, which had been changed in 1956 as a segregationist reaction to the Supreme Court's Brown decision.

For her efforts, Representative Merritt was removed from the committee and the bill was tabled. It was re-introduced in 1972 and defeated, as she was, although narrowly, in her ensuing re-election campaign.

Janet S. Merritt listed the achievements of her legislative career thusly: being a prime instrument in getting the General Civil War engine returned to Georgia from Tennessee as a tourist attraction; having U.S. 19 designated a scenic highway; helping pass legislation that exempted retired civil service employees from certain taxes; working on the Bicentennial Commission appointed by the Speaker of the House; working on the Andersonville Marker

Commission appointed by Governor Jimmy Carter; writing many interim committee reports as chairman; helping with many paving and bridge projects, after approval by proper authorities in Macon, Schley and Sumter; getting surplus property cleared by the highway department for Bel Air Plaza Shopping Center; helping get jobs, scholarships, hardship releases, etc., for constituents; getting peanut facilities for the Plains Experiment Station; working on the State Planning Committee under Elliot Levitas and examining planned communities both in and out of the state; getting facilities through the Appropriations Committee for what was then South Georgia Technical School and Georgia Southwestern College.

After her death at her home on July 23, 2000, her daughter Jane organized and compiled her copious records and correspondence, including audio recordings of interviews and campaign advertisements and jingles, as well as photographs. In February 2004, the Richard B. Russell Library for Political Research and Studies, at the University of Georgia, announced the collection's availability for historical research. One of the library's appropriately female archivists told Jane, "This was a woman of substance." A woman of substance, indeed.

# Speaker Charles Frederick Crisp

It was no coincidence that General Philip Cook would be followed to the United States Congress by his law partner and fellow Confederate veteran, Charles Frederick Crisp. The general feeling among the Bourbon Democrats of the then Third Congressional District viewed the latter worthy gentleman as a natural successor. In 1882 there was no doubt in anyone's mind, as all knew of Charles F. Crisp's superior intellect, political acumen and oratorical skills.

But, I get ahead of myself. Let us, gentle reader, start at the beginning.

Charles Frederick Crisp was born on January 29, 1845, in Sheffield, England. His parents, William Henry and Elizabeth Crisp, were actors and natives of Great Britain who had become naturalized Americans. While on a return trip to the land of their nativity, their son was born and within the year they came back to the former colonies to resume their theatrical schedule.

Because his parents owned several theaters in the region, young Charles was largely educated in the common schools of Georgia, in Macon and Savannah, during the 1850s.

When the tocsin of war sounded in April 1861, the family had settled in Ellaville, where they bought a farm. Sixteen-year-old

Charles was attending school at Luray, Virginia, in the Shenandoah Valley. Ever the patriot of the South, he enlisted the following month in the Tenth Virginia Infantry and was later commissioned a first lieutenant in Company K. He served under General Robert E. Lee until May 12, 1864, when he was captured at the battle of Spotsylvania. He would remain a prisoner of war for the next thirteen months, being incarcerated variously at Fort Delaware, Morris Island in Charleston harbor, Fort Pulaski at Savannah, Hilton Head, and ultimately returned to Fort Delaware. A book, *The Immortal Six Hundred*, was later written about the officers imprisoned at Morris Island.

Upon his return to his parents in Ellaville, Charles F. Crisp decided on a career in law and was admitted to the bar in Americus in 1866.

He also married a year later to Clara Belle Burton, daughter of Colonel Robert Burton, Ellaville's founder, the town having been named for her sister. Previously, it had been known as Pond Town. To this union were born Leila, who married Daniel Frederick Davenport; Berta, who married Carr Sullivan Glover; and sons Frederick and Charles Robert, the last of whom would follow in his father's footsteps as a U.S. Congressman.

In 1872, C.F. Crisp was appointed solicitor-general (now district attorney) for the Southwestern Judicial Circuit and permanently moved his family to Americus in March 1873. Three years later, he completed the two-story frame house at what is now 228 Taylor Street, occupied in recent years by Reverend and Mrs. Frank Kirkland. The Crisp family resided there until 1893. In that year, he built the house at 139 Taylor Street that has a large historic marker in front of it, although it inaccurately claims the house's construction was in the previous decade. The home is now owned and occupied by his great-great-grandson and namesake, Charles Frederick Crisp II.

Charles F. Crisp's political career took off like a rocket after his arrival in Americus. He was re-appointed to a full four-year term as solicitor-general in 1873. Four years later, in June

1894 photo of Speaker Crisp home on Taylor Street the year after he had it built.

1877, he was appointed judge of the superior court of the Southwestern Judicial Circuit, elected by the General Assembly to the same office in 1878, and re-elected judge for a term of four years in 1880.

In September 1882, Charles F. Crisp resigned his judgeship to accept the Democratic nomination for U.S. Congress, to which he was easily elected in November. Taking office on March 4, 1883, he would remain there until his death in 1896. While a Congressman, C.F. Crisp was a strong supporter of the Interstate Commerce Act and an advocate of silver during the great economic debates over the gold standard that dominated national politics at the end of that century. He was chairman of the Committee on Elections in the Fiftieth Congress and the Committee on Rules in the Fifty-second and Fifty-third Congresses.

One of Charles F. Crisp's greatest accomplishments in his distinguished political career was his election over fellow Georgia Democrat Thomas E. Watson as Speaker of the U.S. House of

Representatives in 1891. He was one of only three Georgians so honored, the other two being Democrat Howell Cobb (1849–51), Miss Sarah Cobb's grandfather, and Republican Newt Gingrich (1995–98). C.F. Crisp lost the speakership with the return of Republican control of the U.S. Congress in 1895.

During 1890, Congressman Crisp was involved in two significant events at home in Americus. In February, President Benjamin Harrison appointed one of the black leaders of the local Republican Party, David A. Dudley, as postmaster for the city, a position based then on political patronage. The strenuous objections of Congressman Crisp and the local Democratic power structure successfully killed the nomination. Coincidentally, the Congressman was able to secure financing for a new U.S. Post Office building on Forsyth Street, which became the Bank of Commerce in 1910. For more than half a century it would be run by the Crisp and Sheffield families and their business partners. The Speaker's grandson, Charles F. Crisp II, was the president from 1936 until his retirement. The building was extensively remodeled in 1937 and 1961 and is now the home of Wachovia Bank.

When John B. Gordon resigned his United States Senate seat in 1896, Charles F. Crisp was finally able to realize one of his greatest dreams at the pinnacle of his long commitment to public service. Despite failing health, he conducted an arduous campaign and won the state primary handily in the fall. While awaiting confirmation by the General Assembly, as senators were not popularly elected in those days, Charles Frederick Crisp sought medical treatment in Atlanta where he died suddenly on October 23, 1896, at 1:45 p.m.

A memorial adopted by a mass meeting of the black community at Big Bethel Baptist Church characterized Charles F. Crisp thusly:

> *As a lawyer he stood amid the foremost in his profession; as a judge he was austere yet mild; as a legislator he was ever watchful of the interests of his constituents and did all in his power for Georgia and the nation…as a man he was gentle, tender hearted*

*and kind, and while we all miss his presence his life is one grand
example of triumphs and success.*

It was signed by the most prominent members of that commu-
nity: Dr. A.L. Smith, Charles J. Russell, D.A. Dudley, J.W. Russell,
Reverend A.S. Staley, J.H. Hopkins, Matt Hart, Professor C.A.
Catledge, B.W. Warren and J.H. Covington.

The funeral write-up in the *Times-Recorder* of October 27 paid
eloquent homage to the great man. An abridged version reads as
follows:

*Honored in life, the honors shown Charles F. Crisp in death
have never before been witnessed in Georgia. Fully 5,000 people
witnessed with bowed heads and heavy hearts the last sad rites.
Everyone in Americus paid this deserved tribute to the illustrious dead, while from Atlanta, Macon, Augusta, Columbus, and
from every town and hamlet in the Third congressional district,
came delegations of citizens to attend the obsequies. Every class
of people, from the state's chief executive to the humblest laborer,
crowded about the bier and shed tears of sorrow as they gazed
for the last time upon their honored leader.*

*The remains were accompanied here by Gov. Atkinson and
staff…Hon. Hoke Smith, ex-Secretary of the Interior, ex-
Senator Patrick Walsh of Augusta, Congressmen Chas. L.
Bartlett, Charles L. Moses, E.B. Lewis and J.C.C. Black, ex-
Congressman Barnes, a military escort of commissioned officers
of the Fifth Georgia regiment, the state judiciary, members of the
state senate and house of representatives…*

*The several ministers of the city occupied seats in the pul-
pit, and after the reading of passages of scripture by Revs.
Henderson [Presbyterian] and Christian [Methodist], a
most beautiful and fervent prayer was offered by Rev. Dr. John
B. Turpin [Baptist].*

*General Clement A. Evans arose and delivered the funeral
oration…As a comrade in arms in Virginia, and a close friend in*

*time of peace, he knew well the worth and character of the man he eulogized. His reference to the eminence Mr. Crisp attained in his congressional career was free from any display of fulsome laudation, but was in that simplicity which always marked the even tenor of the life of the man Georgia mourns. No higher tribute could be paid a national character, nor is there one who more just deserved it.*

*"The finest instance of political self denial," said he, "which the country has seen was that furnished in the action of Mr. Crisp when declining the senatorship when it was offered him by Governor Northen. It had been the ambition of his life to fill the seat of senator. This crowning honor was in his grasp, yet at the prompting of duty he put aside the senatorial toga and fulfilled the functions of the office which he was filling. His own action robbed him of the senatorial crown once; death robbed him of it a second time."*

*The casket was borne from the [Methodist] church by the pallbearers, Judge W.H. Fish, Col. E.A. Hawkins, Judge Allen Fort, Hon. W.M. Hawkes, John W. Wheatley, Dr. G.T. Miller, Hon. J.H. Black and Dr. E.J. Eldridge.*

*Arriving at Oak Grove Cemetery the military opened ranks and stood at "present arms." The remains were carried to the family burying lot. A prayer was said by Gen. Evans and the body of the dead statesman was lowered into the grave to sleep beneath the sod of Georgia soil, under southern skies, in the city he loved and the section he served…It remains only to say that Americus feels her great loss and is proud of the honors thus paid her illustrious dead.*

The Speaker's son, Charles R. Crisp, who had been admitted to the Georgia bar the previous year, finished out the three months left in his father's congressional term. He had already served as parliamentarian of the U.S. Congress during the elder Crisp's speakership. In 1898, he had returned to Americus where he married Lucy Sheffield, daughter of John W. Sheffield. After a stint as city court judge (1900–1911), he returned to Washington, D.C., and again served as congressional parliamentarian. At the Democratic National Convention in Baltimore in 1912 he rendered a parliamentary decision that led directly to the nomination of Woodrow Wilson.

That same year, Charles R. Crisp was elected to the congressional district formerly represented by his father. Over the next two decades he would ascend to the chairmanship of the powerful Ways and Means Committee. Carrying on a family tradition in 1932, C.R. Crisp closed out his political career by securing the addition of the third floor to the Americus post office (now the Municipal Building) but, unlike his father, ran an unsuccessful race for the U.S. Senate, losing to Richard B. Russell Jr. Charles Robert Crisp died on February 7, 1937.

# Nineteenth-Century
# Neighborhoods of Americus

What do all the following names have in common: Brooklyn Heights, East Americus, Isomville, Leeton, Lesterville, Prospect Heights? They are all names of neighborhoods and suburbs of Americus. Actually, Brooklyn and Prospect Heights was essentially the same place, just different names.

The oldest of these was East Americus, settled in the 1830s by families, among whom were my ancestors. It encompassed the area including Cherry, Crawford, Elmo, Forsyth, Hudson, Jefferson, Lamar, Mayo, Oglethorpe and Rees. Families named Blalock, Cobb, Castleberry, Gunn, Hudson, Mathews, Mayo, Smith, Speer and Sullivan lived there well into the twentieth century. Two are memorialized in street names, John J. Hudson and David A. Mayo, both having served on the city council (the former 1877–80 and the latter in 1867). In fact, over a hundred years ago virtually the entire city police force resided in East Americus.

The Methodists of the neighborhood started the second church of that denomination in the city, originally East Americus Methodist in 1879, at the southwest corner of Hudson and Jefferson. In 1894, the church was renamed St. Paul's and moved to the southwest corner of Jefferson and Mayo. In 1914, when W.H.C. Wheatley bought the property where Sumter Regional Hospital is now

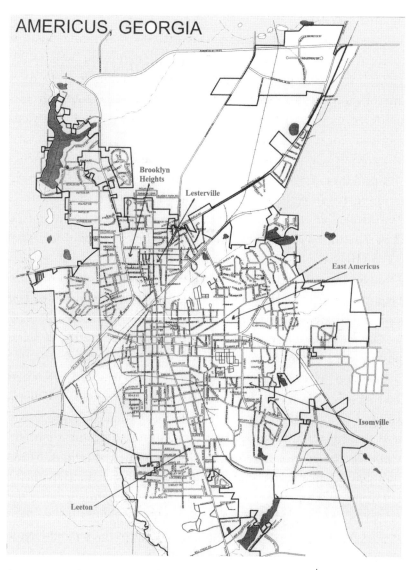

Americus map showing nineteenth-century neighborhoods.

located, the church was moved to the northwest corner of Lamar and Rees, ending its days with the Primitive Baptists. The lot has been occupied in recent decades by the city's oldest insurers, the Baldwin Agency.

One neighborhood, Leeton, was actually a separate political entity. Chartered by an act of the state legislature on January 20, 1872, it was located on South Lee Street, stretching from Dodson on the north to the former country club on the south. It was bordered on the east by Elm Avenue. In this part of Americus there were no streets west of Lee at that time. Leeton was named in honor of General Robert E. Lee and its first city council was comprised of John V. Price, Robert R. Brown, Dr. William N.L. Crocker, Frank E. Burke and the intendant, or mayor, Robert T. Byrd. Intendant Byrd had built his home in 1870 and it yet stands, known to the city's oldest residents as the Judge Hixon place, now owned by R.E. "Bobby" Monahan Jr. His grandfather was John F. Monahan, a charter member and later chief of the Americus Fire Department. F.E. Burke's home was at the northeast corner of Lee and his namesake, now the Lee Street Methodist Church parking lot. Another Leetonian, James E. Bivins, had a home on Elm facing the street named for his family.

Leeton gave up its charter in April 1885 and was reincorporated into Americus proper. The name remained for some years thereafter, as in 1890 when the electric streetcar route went there and Major William L. Glessner, a veteran of the "Late Unpleasantness" and owner of the *Americus Recorder*, built the Victorian house at the southeast corner of Lee and the street that now bears his name.

During the Spanish-American War of 1898, Leeton was the site of a U.S. Army encampment, Camp Gilman, about where Pat's Place is now. The Eighth Massachusetts Infantry and Twelfth New York Infantry were the units stationed there. Charles L. Ansley and one of his sons, while hunting in the woods nearby, found a soldier who had committed suicide by hanging himself from a tree. Another military connection occurred in 1913 when the Americus Light Infantry, the local state militia, established a five hundred-yard shooting range near the former country club on the southern edge of Leeton.

The 1880 federal census of Americus revealed two black neighborhoods here. On the north side was Lesterville, centered around the intersection of North Jackson Street and Lester, from Masonic on the north to Patterson on the south. The street name commemorates the antebellum property of Alfred J. Lester, father-in-law of John T. Windsor, for whom the hotel is named. Families on Lester in the 1891 city directory bore the names Bartlett, Bostic, Causey, Drake, Ellison, Harris, Mons, Sanders, Shockley, Turner, Wade, Williams, Wilson and Woods.

In the city's southeast quadrant, Isomville was located along Tripp Street, from Felder to Parker. The names of the main thoroughfare and neighborhood are derived from the presence of two local residents. Wesley Tripp and his family were there in that 1880 census. A gentleman known to history only as Uncle Isom, a venerated figure in the community, was responsible for the honorific Isomville. Settled by former slaves and those one generation removed from that odious institution, longtime families, many stalwarts of Trinity AME Church (1888–1965), at the northeast corner of Parker and Tripp, included those named Bright, Coleman, Gibson, Holland, Jackson, McGrady, Montgomery, Moore, Ollif, Patterson, Prince, Robinson and Tripp.

Brooklyn Heights began as an antebellum neighborhood just outside the city's original corporate limits, or "across the branch," as the area was known in those days. The first home was built by William Hubert, about where the Tog Shop is presently situated. The family even had a private cemetery there, although the graves were transferred to Oak Grove in 1935 by John Sheffield, who was developing the area. This home became the domicile of Joseph C. Roney, Americus postmaster from 1885 to 1892. The area north of there was known for many years as Roney's Woods and the name still survives in Roney Street.

Judge James P. Guerry of the Inferior Court, predecessor to our county commission, built his home on the west side of Ellaville Road, just north of the intersection with Friendship Road, in the

Dr. R.C. Black's 1857 home in Brooklyn Heights.

1840s. His daughter married Captain John L. Adderton, CSA, for whom the street is named, and their daughter, Mrs. Smithwick, resided in the Guerry house until her death in 1954. John L. Adderton served in the 1880s as our state representative and on the city council. The home site has been replaced by the Gear Master Transmissions complex.

Colonel William J. Patterson, Esquire, erected the third residence there, a seven-room structure on twenty-five acres at the intersection of Ellaville Road and the street named after him. This house burned in 1880 but the family immediately rebuilt. Colonel Patterson was one of three founders of the Americus Presbyterian Church in 1842 and had been the solicitor-general here from 1843 to 1847. We now use the title district attorney for this officer of the court.

On the southeast corner of Lester Street and Ellaville Road, Samuel McGarrah, for whom the entire street was named, constructed his home about 1877. A county commissioner (1874–75), he co-owned a large cotton warehouse where Forsyth now crosses

Cotton Avenue. Former city councilman Jim Littlefield's great-grandfather, Edmund H. Ross, was his brother-in-law.

Walter T. Davenport, longtime pillar of the Americus Methodist Church (now First United Methodist), came to Americus from Virginia about 1840. After briefly residing on Lamar, followed by a tan yard on McGarrah Street, W.T. Davenport bought about eighty acres on the west side of the Ellaville Road. His home, built circa 1856, is the only surviving antebellum structure on the west side of the main thoroughfare. On an overgrown weeded lot, squeezed between a trailer park and an abandoned house next to Fred's Auto Repair, it was last used by Mary Baldwin as an antiques store in the 1980s.

Charles Woodson Coker bought Davenport's tan yard and built his home there about 1853. After the Civil War, he sold the house to Beverly C. Mitchell, whose family members lived in it continuously until the death of Miss Sallie Mitchell in 1942. B.C. Mitchell's son, Frank P. Mitchell, was the Americus postmaster from 1902 to 1913. The family's name is preserved in the street adjoining the property on the southeast.

Reverend Robert J. Hodges, of near Andersonville, began construction of the next house in Brooklyn Heights but sold it in 1857 before completion. Dr. Robert C. Black, mayor of Americus during the Civil War, bought and finished the house, residing in it for more than three decades. Known to many old-timers as the Speer home, the structure was lost to the fire demon in 1969.

The *Times-Recorder* of November 25, 1891, contained an interesting description of another prominent resident of Brooklyn Heights, one of the founders of Scott's Mater Tabernacle CME Church: "Another great character 'over the creek' was old man Riley Covington, the fiddler, the barber, the race rider and last the preacher. Dr. Black gave old man Riley a home for life time and embodied in the deed these words, 'So long as he, Riley, behaves himself and keeps the place of a negro, he shall live on the aforesaid property until his death.' He kept his place and lived a peaceable life, and when he died there were more white people in attendance upon his funeral than there were negroes." For years afterwards, the area behind the Davenport property was known as the old Riley Covington neighborhood. The 1891 city directory listed a Covington Street, which was probably the extension of Davenport Street to Magnolia Street.

When Daniel F. Davenport and Christopher C. Hawkins developed the seventy-acre Dr. Black place in 1890, it acquired the name Brooklyn Heights and the recreational spring across the road was named Prospect Park. D.F. Davenport had been a pharmacy student in New York City and named both areas after their northern counterparts. In 1907, Hugh L. Mize opened Prospect Park with a wooden swimming pool, nature trail and petting zoo.

Thomas J. Baisden Jr., after clerking with W.T. Davenport, bought the lot just south of Davenport's in 1896 and erected the house on the north side of Davenport Street. Badly damaged in a 1936 fire, the V.H. Cavender family had it brick-veneered and it yet overlooks where Baisden Street was, between the old Rib Rack and the new Americus Garden Apartments, the latter obliterating the last vestiges of Baisden Street.

Across Davenport Street, now the Fuller Center for Housing, is the antebellum home of Jesse New, a house painter who built it in 1860. For decades it was a rental property owned by the Mitchell family cited previously. The house was moved twenty feet west in 1934, when Highway 19 was extended from McGarrah Street to the intersection with Highway 280. Thad Allen had it converted into a motor court in 1949. Most current residents will remember it as the Dragon Palace, the city's first Chinese restaurant.

After a yearlong struggle with the city council, the Martin Luther King Jr. Ministerial Association, led by Reverend Fer-Rell Malone of Bethesda Baptist Church, achieved its goal of renaming Highway 19 inside the city limits as Martin Luther King Jr. Boulevard on December 10, 1992. It is now the main thoroughfare of the neighborhood.

All these neighborhoods are now well within the corporate confines of Americus. Each has made its own unique contribution to our city and we are all the better for it.

# "Residenter of 1838"

Major Moses Speer was born on February 17, 1832, in Giles County, Tennessee, the second son of Hugh Lawson and Elender Ann "Helen" Coffman Speer. His older brother, Amos Coffman Speer, was my maternal grandmother's paternal grandfather.

Hugh L. Speer was the second son of Captain Moses Speer and his second wife, Hannah Thompson Lawson, who were married at the home of her father, Roger Lawson, in the then state capital of Louisville on January 4, 1802. Her father, having settled in Queensborough in the mid-1700s on the Ogeechee River, was an officer in the Revolutionary War. Her uncle, Hugh Lawson, was on the committee that selected the site of the University of Georgia in the 1780s.

The major's grandfather, whose patronymic he bore although he was not overly fond of it, was an immigrant from County Antrim in Northern Ireland circa 1770, who located in Alexandria, Virginia, as a merchant and fought throughout the war. He married his first wife, Mary Hall, on April 8, 1794, in Frederick County (now in West Virginia), then migrated to Greene County, Georgia. As one of Greenesboro's first citizens, Captain Speer represented the county in the General Assembly in 1795–96, 1800–04 and again in 1808. He was also sheriff from 1797 to 1799, then coroner from 1799 to 1800. After a brief sojourn in Jasper County, where he was a justice of the peace in 1811, Captain Speer was also a justice of the peace in Morgan County in 1817. He died there in 1824 at the advanced age of seventy-four years.

Hugh L. Speer married Helen Coffman on January 23, 1828, in Jasper County where her parents, Amos and Sarah Coffman, resided before they finally immigrated to Alabama. In 1829 the newlyweds moved to Tennessee. Their return to Georgia in 1837 was recalled by Major Speer when the family was accidentally dumped from their wagon at Gunter's Crossing in northern Alabama. Helen Coffman Speer died July 24, 1837; her youngest child, John Coffman, followed her on August 31 and her brother-in-law, David Speer, in November of the same year.

While settling the estate in Morgan County, young Moses was sent to Sumter County in 1838 to visit his aunt and uncle, Judge William Tinsley and his third wife, the former Margaret Speer, at their plantation on the Starkville Road seven miles south of Americus. For a hundred years beginning in 1874 it was known as the Simpson place, although the house was built by Thomas Dixon Speer, the major's uncle, during the Civil War.

The grieving widower moved with his children, Amos, Moses and Mary Ann (twins) and Louisa to Troup County where he married, on August 15, 1839, Martha Wales Allen Biggs, a widow. They had five children, one of whom, Hugh Lawson, was killed in the Civil War. They immediately moved to near Franklin in Heard County. There, H.L. Speer carried on the family's commitment to public service as the county's sheriff, treasurer, superior court clerk and justice of the inferior court between 1839 and 1854.

When the family moved to Chambers County, Alabama, Moses Speer, who had been a clerk and bookkeeper in a dry goods store in Franklin, went in the opposite direction, not being happy with his stepmother, and arrived in Americus on March 2, 1854. He opened a provisions store with his cousin's husband, Portlock Fowler Thompson, who had just completed his final term as sheriff.

Private Moses Speer of the
Sumter Light Guards in January
1862.

On December 23, 1856, Moses Speer married Bicy M. Hooks, the sister of William Hooks, great-great-grandfather of my friend, Senator George B. Hooks. Their only child, Mary Ella, died at age two and her mother passed away less than a year later on July 31, 1860. Both are buried on the old Bardin Hooks plantation in Macon County.

With the outbreak of the Civil War in 1861, Moses Speer enlisted as a private in the Sumter Light Guards, Company K, Fourth Georgia Regiment. He fought valiantly until the battle of Malvern Hill on July 1, 1862, when he was shot in the mouth, the bullet exiting behind his ear. Left on the battlefield for dead overnight, his life was saved by the timely arrival of his uncle, T.D. Speer, who brought him from Virginia to the latter's newly built home, Liberty Hall, on the old Tinsley place.

After a complete recovery, including the growth of a beard to cover the scarring, on February 10, 1863, Moses Speer married Laura Hicks Cowles, daughter of Asbury and Caroline Bonner Cowles. To this union were born May, Ernest, Eustace Asbury, Caroline Bonner and Robert Hugh. The eldest daughter married Charles L. Ansley, Eustace moved to Atlanta, Carrie, a Wesleyan graduate, never married and Ernest and Robert died young.

In August 1863 Moses Speer re-enlisted as a second lieutenant in Company A, Fifth Battalion, Georgia Infantry, State Guards, and rose to the rank of major on the staff of General Henry K. McCay during the battle of Atlanta in the summer of 1864. The family is in possession of a letter he wrote from the porch at Ponder's House.

The following summer in 1865 found Major Speer taking four wagons of cotton overland to Savannah, investing in a mixed stock of goods, and returning to Americus, where he ran a successful brokerage and insurance agency along with his brother-in-law, Joseph J. Granberry. They were located in the building constructed by the latter gentleman in 1850, known for the rest of that century as Granberry's Corner, now Kinnebrew's, the oldest surviving brick structure in the city. Coincidentally, Major Speer built, in 1868–69, the first brick residence in Americus, one block away at the northeast corner of Church and Jackson. It was razed in 1939 with the bricks being used in the construction of the gas station that replaced it on the site. Two of its most famous guests were Georgia humorist Bill Arp in 1880 and Governor Alexander H. Stephens in 1882.

Following in the footsteps of his father and grandfather, M. Speer (his preferred signature) served in public office as the county treasurer from 1863 to 1870. During his half century of residency he also organized, and later served as president of, the Americus Library Association in 1878. When the Americus city school sys-

Major M. Speer family portrait circa 1896 on the steps of the first brick home built in Americus. *Left to right*: Major Speer, Mrs. M. Speer, Eustace S. Ansley, Miss Mary Granberry, J.J. Granberry, E.A. Speer, Mrs. E.A. Speer, Charles S. Ansley, Miss Carrie Speer, Miss Rebecca Cowles, Charles L. Ansley, Mrs. C.L. Ansley.

tem was chartered in 1873, M. Speer was a member of that first board and, after the schools began operating in 1880, he was the board treasurer for many years. During the seven years of debate over the Americus schools, much of it based on race, Major Speer made this prescient observation: "as we educate the negro and lift him up to a higher plane, will crime be diminished and taxation reduced...we are only helping ourselves after all, when we contribute to the moral and mental culture of the negro race. Of two things we should choose, to make the negro better, or to banish him from the land. We cannot afford to do the latter, then let us do the former with cheerful hearts and willing hands, for jails and courthouses are more expensive than school houses."

A pillar of the now First United Methodist Church, M. Speer played an integral role in the Sunday school movement, attending as a delegate the International Conventions in London, England, in 1889 and in Pittsburgh, Pennsylvania, in 1890. Largely self-taught since he had grown up with only the "benefit of a few month's schooling," as a Shakespearean scholar he made side trips to Stratford-upon-Avon and to Paris during the 1889 convention. At the latter's exposition, the major and his daughter, Carrie, witnessed the grand opening of the Eiffel Tower. Brother-in-law J.J. Granberry had been the first superintendent of the Methodist Sunday school in 1849 at the church's original location on the northeast corner of Church and Prince. Three Methodist bishops, Pierce, Doggett and Candler, along with virtually every visiting and resident preacher were guests in his home. Ironically, the split that had made the Methodists un-united occurred after the Georgia Conference's last session in Americus in 1866, attended by M. Speer and J.J. Granberry.

Major M. Speer amassed a considerable fortune and became one of the city's premier capitalists. With his brother-in-law, William Hooks, he organized the first banking business in Americus. From 1865 to 1870 they operated under the firm names of Adams, Speer & Co., Granberry, Speer & Co., and Speer & Hooks. In 1870 the Bank of Americus was chartered with Francis M. Coker, of the Plains of Dura, and M. Speer as cashier. Major Speer became president of that institution in 1882 until he formed his own, the Bank of Southwestern Georgia, in 1887. It was located in the Thomas Block on the northwest corner of Forsyth and Jackson. Ill health forced the major's retirement in 1896.

In the interim, beginning in 1888, Major Speer led the city's capitalists in the formation two years later of a syndicate, the Americus Manufacturing and Improvement Corporation, which built the city's most identifiable landmark, the Windsor Hotel. The incorporators, at $10,000 each, were S.H. Hawkins, M. Speer, J.W. Sheffield, P.C. Clegg, Glover & Lanier, T. Wheatley, C.M. Wheatley, John Windsor, C.C. Hawkins and W.E. Hawkins.

After an illness of two years, his life well spent, Major Moses Speer succumbed on December 10, 1898, at his home. The services were held at his beloved Methodist Church and the pallbearers, R.J. Perry, E.J. Eldridge, U.B. Harrold, John W. Wheatley, W.H.C.

Dudley, W.M. Jones, P.H. Williams, J.W. Sheffield, W.T. Davenport and Arthur Rylander, were Americus's most prominent citizens, attesting to the esteem in which Major Moses Speer was held.

# Political Firsts

Our first state representative in 1832, John W. Cowart, super-vised the surveying of the courthouse square for the new county seat. The first woman elected to the legislature from Sumter County was not until Mrs. Janet Burton Scarborough Merritt accomplished that feat 133 years later! Our first state senator, Lovett B. Smith, served concurrently as our first county treasurer. He sponsored the legislation that chartered Americus and he also gave it that name. Lovett B. Smith served, as well, as first justice of the peace for the 789th GMD, which encompasses Americus and its environs. The county treasurer was the first public office to which a woman, Mrs. Erin Watts Stewart, was elected. That event transpired in 1926. Our first sheriff, John Kimmey, was mur-dered in December 1839 (where the Byne Block now stands at the northwest corner of Forsyth and Lee) during a disagreement with George W. Robinson, his political opponent whom he killed in self-defense. Ironically, only three years earlier the two had served side by side as first and second lieutenants in the Sumter Cavalry under Captain Isaac McCrary in the wars with the Lower Creek Indians.

My great-great-great-grandfather, Jacob W. Cobb, did double duty as the county's first superior court clerk and county ordinary;

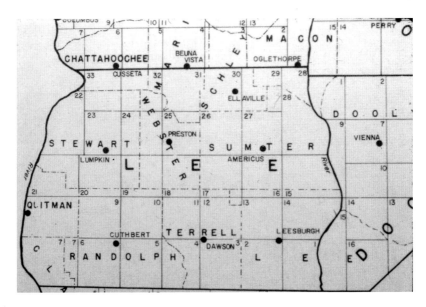

Original boundaries of Lee County, from the Flint River on the east to the Chattahoochee River on the west.

the latter official we now call probate judge. As the superior court clerk, it was his office in the antebellum courthouse that was ransacked by the farmers' mob that kidnapped the deputy sheriff to prevent public sales of their land in May 1842. That deputy was the aforementioned Isaac McCrary.

Our first inferior court judges, precursors to our modern county commissioners, were John J. Britt, Thomas D. Harvey, Richard Salter, Robert Savage and Benjamin Strange. They established the routes of the highways that now crisscross Sumter County. J.J. Britt built the first sawmill here to produce the lumber for our first courthouse, which was located in the middle of the town square, now bisected by Windsor Avenue. The county inferior courts were abolished in 1868 by the Reconstruction constitution and our first county commission in 1872 consisted of James H. Black, James W. Furlow, Samuel Heys, Amos K. Schumpert and Seth K. Taylor. Sam Heys, an English immigrant, was the general contractor who built the Furlow Masonic Female College, as well as the stockade

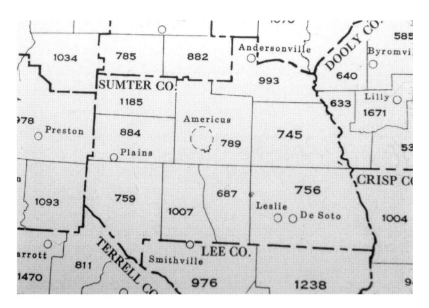

Georgia Militia Districts in Sumter County, including Americus, Andersonville, DeSoto, Leslie, and Plains.

at Camp Sumter, better known to history as Andersonville Prison. Taylor Street is named for the family of S.K. Taylor, whose home was at the southwest corner of Barlow and Taylor. The first black person, Arthur C. Pless, would not be elected to the county commission until eleven decades later, in 1981.

Our first tax receiver, Jacob Little, was notorious for his lax bookkeeping practices, sometimes writing receipts on whatever scraps of paper were available at that moment. He often carried out his duties barefooted. It was in this office, in 1925, that Mrs. Emma Joiner became the first woman to hold public office in the county's history, following the death of the incumbent, George D. Jones. The position was abolished in 1928 with Mrs. Nannie Dodson Britton completing the last year of the term of her late husband, John R. Britton. On a personal note, my great-great-grandfather, James A. Daniel, held that office from 1875 until his death in 1887. Incidentally, my other great-great-grandfather, Amos C. Speer, held three separate political positions: tax collector

(1871–78), ordinary judge (1885–1900) and county treasurer (1903–07). Both were maimed Confederate veterans, each having sacrificed a leg in their Lost Cause.

The first mayor of Americus, Perry H. Oliver (1856–57), was a Savannah businessman originally from Macon. He toured the nation for three years afterwards as manager of the musical prodigy Blind Tom, a former slave born near Columbus. In 1860 they put on a concert at Willard Hall in Washington, D.C., to honor the first Japanese delegation to the United States. The first city council consisted of Wade J. Barlow, Angus D. Bruce, James G. McCrary, Alfred F. McPherson, John E. Sullivan and William T. Toole. Green M. Wheeler, having already served several terms as sheriff, was the first city clerk. Over two hundred individual citizens have served on that august body, including its first black members, Mrs. Eloise Richardson Paschal and Mrs. Eddie Rhea Ross Walker, beginning in 1996. The city's first marshal, William D. McKay, was responsible for overseeing the establishment of Oak Grove Cemetery in 1857.

After a half-century, our first neighbors became incorporated in 1881, when Andersonville (originally Anderson Station) elected its first mayor, Elder Thomas K. Pursley, who was seventy-one years old. With the extension of Samuel H. Hawkins's railroad in the mid-1880s, DeSoto was incorporated in November 1889, with Edward S. Ferguson as its first mayor. His grandson, Woodrow Wilson "Billy" Ferguson, served on the county commission from 1963 to 1998. Immediately west of DeSoto, Leslie was first named Job due to a clerical error in Washington, D.C., when its post office was commissioned. Founder James W. Bailey had submitted the name Jeb for his father's initials, J.E. Bailey. The citizens petitioned the state legislature for a name change in August 1887 and two years later, in September 1889, the town was rechristened for J.W. Bailey's daughter, Leslie. It was officially chartered by the state legislature in December 1892. A post office was established in September 1839 at the Plains of Dura in the western portion of Sumter County. Postmaster David W. Robinet named it for the Old Testament location outside of

Babylon because of the community's sectarian dispute among its three Protestant denominations. As Hawkins's railroad extended west in 1884, the town moved a mile to its present location and was renamed simply Plains. Its first city council in January 1897 was led by Dr. Burr T. Wise as mayor, with Randolphus S. Oliver, William L. Thomas, Edwin Timmerman Sr. and Luther D. Wise as councilmen. Over a hundred years later, many of those families are still well represented in that historic community.

There are many interesting facts about our local elected officials over the years. The Honorable William Adolphus Dodson, for whom the street is named, was Speaker Pro Tem of the Georgia House of Representatives in 1896–97. State Senator William Harris Crawford Wheatley arranged for the establishment here of what is now Georgia Southwestern State University during his term in 1905–06. William Adams Wilson was senate president pro tem in 1892–93. W.A. Dodson moved from the house to the senate and served as its president in 1898–99. As the youngest member of the general assembly in 1873, Allen Fort wrote the law creating the Americus city school system, which served the community with distinction until December 1994. All were residents of Americus.

I'll conclude this effort with my personal favorite, the coroner's office. Its first occupant, Larkin Glover, was the patriarch of a large family that has remained prominent throughout the county's history. Two of his successors, however, really had to overcome obstacles to perform their duties. William Walter Guerry, who served from 1868 until his death in 1884, had lost both his arms in a childhood accident and was known locally as "No-arm Bill." Despite his handicap, W.W. Guerry married, raised a family and was completely self-sufficient. Edd Jenkins, of Leslie, who was coroner from 1909 to 1952, was totally blind. I still have not figured out how he pulled off that feat.

As you read this today, please make sure that all of you who are registered exercise the suffrage guaranteed for you by the sacrifices of our patriotic forebears. It is the least you can do as a beneficiary of the world's greatest democracy.